HEALING PRAYER

With Daily Prayers For A Month

by

WILLIAM PORTSMOUTH, M.A

I will pray with the understanding also.

ARTHUR JAMES LIMITED
THE DRIFT, EVESHAM, WORCS.

© Arthur James Ltd. 1954

First published 1954
Second edition 1955
Third edition 1957
Fourth edition 1960
Fifth edition 1963
Sixth edition 1967
Seventh edition 1974

First paperback edition 1980
Reprinted 1984

ISBN 0 85305 230 1

Made and printed in Great Britain by
Purnell and Sons (Book Production) Ltd.,
Member of the BPCC Group, Paulton, Bristol

For Elsie, whose understanding
love is itself a healing grace.

O Lord, support us all the day long of this troublous life, until the shades lengthen, the evening comes, the busy world is hushed, the fever of life is over and our work is done. Then, Lord, in Thy mercy grant us safe lodging, a holy rest and peace at the last, through Jesus Christ our Lord. Amen.

FOREWORD

By the BISHOP OF WORCESTER

THE Rev. William Portsmouth gives us here a book, both thoughtful and challenging, simple and practical, written out of his wide experience as vicar of a parish. It carries with it a note of reality and makes us face facts and study its principles of the devotional life.

Healing Prayer is divided into two main sections. In the first the author deals with divine healing, based on the fact that God neither wills nor sends disease. To this is linked a careful examination of the underlying factors of our prayer life. In the second half of the book we are given carefully chosen prayers for each day, morning and evening, for a month.

I commend this book particularly to clergy and ministers, and of course with special emphasis on those who work among sick and suffering people in hospitals and other places. It gives us a balanced relationship between the medical profession and the Christian minister, between the prayer of faith that brings healing and the skill of doctors and nurses.

Here there is no clash of interest. Whether it is always recognised or not, the real point is that God works through the normal activities of trained members of the medical profession, and God certainly answers prayer. It is increasingly recognised that the spiritual cannot be left out in the care of the suffering, any more than the medical or surgical can be ignored. Chaplain and doctor find common ground in the faith that God cares and wills healing and health to His children.

WILLIAM WORCESTER.

Hartlebury Castle
Kidderminster,
Worcestershire.

PREFACE

THIS LITTLE BOOK of prayers has been prepared primarily for use by the sick and those who minister to them, at home or in hospital. But I hope it may be of value to many others. It is designed to encourage a healthy attitude in prayer, so that its usefulness need not be limited to the sick.

The prayers have all been written on the assumption, amply warranted in Scripture, that God is ever at work for good, round us and in us. Our praying is, therefore, far more satisfying and strengthening to us when it can express grateful and joyful acknowledgement of God's present goodness than when it is anxiously beseeching for absent mercies. What is offered here is, in fact, a book of Affirmative Healing Prayer.

It is not necessary to be a theologian in order to pray, yet all real prayer must have a theology. Jesus has revealed God to us most clearly, and out of that revelation comes His teaching on the right way to approach God in prayer.

The Lord's Prayer is the classic example of affirmative prayer. It begins with the assumption that God is good. It seeks the spread of a Kingdom already existing. It lays our needs quite trustfully before God without dwelling anxiously upon them; and, acknowledging that the Kingdom is already in God's safe hands, is content at the end to say triumphantly "Amen", "So be it", which is not a request, but an affirmation.

It is this kind of attitude which informs all the prayers that follow. Their theology is that of the Lord's Prayer. If we adopt this attitude, we shall find that anxious petition will give way to grateful acceptance, despairing appeals to joyful acknowledgement. Instead of praying with shallow optimism we shall pray with triumphant affirmation. We shall come, not to beg, but to receive.

The silent meditations provided for each day represent another expression of the same affirmative attitude.

These forms of prayer make much room for thanksgiving and joyfulness. Petition is by no means excluded, for we are taught by Scripture to bring our needs to God, but there is not, nor ought there to be, any note of anxiety in it.

*   *   *   *   *

I have myself found affirmative prayer to be a most satisfying means of communion with God, both in sickness and in health. There are many people who can testify to the blessings they have experienced, in body, mind and soul, by reason of the affirmative attitude, supported, as of course it must be, by a simple, positive faith. For me, this way of prayer has never grown stale. I find that its value increases as time goes on. It opens the gates of the heart to the life and health and goodness which God is ever waiting to pour into us, once we have swept away the barrier of fear and doubt and anxiety, and other negative, harmful emotions.

I have not striven for literary excellence in the prayers I have written. God is a searcher of the heart before He is a literary critic. It is the attitude of mind which counts, whether we use a devotional classic or merely struggle over our own words. I cannot say that I have written the prayers on my knees, but I have used them thus to find that they do express satisfyingly what is in my heart. The forms suggested are offered only as guides and helps, and are meant primarily for personal rather than corporate use, though some of them I have used during intercessions in church. If the book is able to help any who use it to draw near to God in their prayer time with a deeper sense of His healing and strengthening nearness, I shall be sufficiently rewarded.

*   *   *   *   *

I owe my thanks to the Rev. Jim Wilson, Chaplain of the Guild of Health, and to Miss M. V. Dunlop, of the Fellowship of Meditation, for reading the typescript, and for various useful suggestions. It is right to record here a heavy debt of gratitude to both these people for all that I have learned from them about healing prayer. Without them this book could never have been written. All faults and imperfections in the following pages, however, must be placed against my own account.

It has not been possible in my limited space to deal more fully with the subjects of affirmative prayer and meditation. Those who would learn more will find much useful material in such books as *Healing Through the Power of Christ,* by Jim Wilson, and two booklets by Miss M. V. Dunlop, *Contemplative Meditation and Stillness and Strength.* The Rev. W. Mauleverer's book *A New Way to Pray* will also be found most helpful. All these can be obtained from the Guild of Health, Edward Wilson House, 26 Queen Anne Street, Harley Street, London, W.1.

I am grateful, too, to the publishers, Arthur James Ltd., for their kind co-operation, as well as for all they do to stimulate the work of Christian Healing.

W. P.

The Vicarage,
    Birtley,
        Co. Durham.

CONTENTS

PART I

I

PRAYING FOR HEALTH

As the preface indicates, this book is intended for use by sick people who long to recover their health, as well as by those who wish to pray for the sick. But it is hoped that praying for healing will not cease when health has been restored. If prayer can bring about health it can also maintain it, and that is surely a desirable object at all times.

Before starting a course of prayer for healing we ought to try to understand what we mean by the word *health*. Most people think of it as a state of physical well-being. On this understanding, a person who has no physical ailments is regarded as *healthy*. But the human personality comprises more than flesh and blood. This obvious fact is too often overlooked in the search for health, with disastrous consequences. The personality is a close-knit union of body, mind and soul, delicately and inextricably related to each other. To seek perfection for one element of personality at the expense of the others is to do damage to the whole.

Body, mind and soul are an entity. They cannot be arbitrarily separated, for they constantly inter-act upon each other, however vaguely we may be aware of the fact. A sick body can depress the soul and warp the judgment. A sick mind, or even a period of morbid or unhappy thoughts, can, and does, produce physical change, often of a serious nature. The mental attitude has the capacity, also, for affecting the soul, both adversely and otherwise. Likewise the soul of man may inform the mind with a knowledge beyond the range of sense, and give to the body powers of endurance and recuperation outside of apparent physical possibility. *The soul of man is capable of intuitions which transcend mental processes, and can lend wings to a tortured frame.*

If we admit all this, it will be obvious that the desire for healing is to be understood in terms far wider than those of mere physical well-being. True healing is the process which aims at the perfection of all three, simply because they are not really three, but one.

If we really wish for health, we must seek for, and desire with a great desire, the healing of the whole man, the total personality. To seek less than this is to misunderstand the meaning of the word "health". That word could, without damage to its meaning, be spelled "whole-th", for that is what fulness of health is—*wholeness.*

Our praying, then, will be for wholeness, the healing of the total personality. In doing so we shall be bringing ourselves more into line with the purpose and will of God, to Whom we pray. And we shall see, moreover, that the health we are seeking is not only our own, but that of all men. We shall be lifted out of ourselves, and all our self-concern, and become identified with the grand, over-all Divine objective of world-redemption.

*   *   *   *   *

This understanding of "health" gives fresh meaning to the familiar but much misunderstood word "salvation". This word has been battered about, mishandled and abused in a long and regrettable history of popular theological exposition until now it conveys to the untutored scarcely anything of the great Biblical vision of a humanity completely restored in all its parts, perfected with the perfection of God Himself, until it glistens with the glory of the Creator.

Now it is true that from the Christian viewpoint the spirit of man is of more than mortal stuff, and that in our next stage of existence, after physical death, we shall not have a body like the present one. Nevertheless in this world we have a body, by means of which the spirit expresses itself. And if God made this body, it is part of His purpose that it should also be *saved*.

"Salvation" is the English translation of the Latin word "salus", meaning "health", itself translated from the Greek "soteria", meaning "keeping alive", "preserving". And it was for salvation that Jesus came into the world. He came to save, to give health to, to preserve alive, the whole man. Just as we must not think of health as only a physical condition, so we must not confine it to a spiritual condition, to be enjoyed only after physical death. *God intends us to have healthy souls and bodies here on earth.*

This is the Christian message of hope, distinguishing it from all other religions. Jesus, it is written, came that we might have *life,* and have it abundantly, that is, in all its fulness. He came that we might have life. What life?

There is only one real life, the life of God. God is life and the giver of it. Since He is eternal, that life exists now. Jesus meant that He came to enable us to enter into that life *now*. When we have come to know, and accept, the truth as it is in Jesus, we have entered into *knowledge of salvation*. Jesus by His perfect life demonstrated God in all His fulness. The Incarnation was an invasion into history on the part of God Himself. *The Word became flesh*. This does not mean that God reduced Himself to a low level merely to share our condition as an example, but rather that by taking flesh He raised humanity to His own level, to enable it to rise above its apparent limitations. And the prospect laid before us by union with Him is not to be thought of in terms of becoming super-human, but in terms of the possibility of being raised from our present sub-human state to that of true humanity as God meant it to be, the Humanity of the Word-made-flesh.

Because of His perfect humanity, Jesus never had a disease, never did sin, and was in perfect control of His environment, calming a storm, walking on the water, rising from death. By His words and works He brought to people an actual experience of God's power round them and in them, for without doubt He conveyed the actualities of spiritual and physical healing. His taking of the Cross, the symbol of the world's desperate sickness of body and soul, and His triumphant defeat of it demonstrated for all time the certainty of God's saving power.

Moreover, He made clear, with a clarity that has been shining down the ages in the lives of His people, that the means whereby we enter into the experience of life, salvation, and health, is faith in God as revealed in Him: "This is life eternal, that they know thee, the only real God, and him whom thou hast sent, even Jesus Christ" (St. John 17: 3—Moffatt).

*   *   *   *   *

Faith is *the substance of things hoped for, the evidence of things unseen*. That is to say, it is the grasping hold of, and making our very own, the knowledge that God is, and that Jesus has declared Him; that is, made Him plain before our eyes. By faith we enter into life, into salvation, into health. The true basis of all health is, in fact, spiritual.

Fulness of life begins with an inner relationship with the Giver of Life. It is by means of this relationship of spirit that the mind is informed with truth, and that the body, in turn, by its actions and reactions, reveals that truth physically.

A medical psychologist has written: "Error creeps in (in the practice of medicine) when due recognition is not given to the other aspects of the personality. The physical is dominated by the mental, and this in turn by the spiritual. Whether we admit it or not, the spirit of man is a major factor in all illness."

As, then, we enter into prayer with the Author of Life in order that we, or other people, might recover health, we must bear these things in mind. We are to seek for fulness of health in spirit, mind and body now, not in some distant hereafter. Our objective is that the whole personality might enter into life in this world, that it may be the better fitted to continue it in the next with whatever means of expression God has there provided for it.

It might be asked, if we can enter into a health-giving union with God by the prayer of faith, what is the place of the Sacraments? There is, indeed, a place for the Sacraments in the restoration of humanity to fulness of life with God, and each Sacrament has a healing value all its own. But the Sacraments can have but little value if they are not sustained by inner conviction. And inner conviction is a highly individual affair. It is with the inner life, the prayer-life, of the individual that we are here concerned, the individual who is prepared to accept the truth of God as Christ has revealed Him.

The Sacraments cannot be studied apart from the corporate nature of the Church, and that is beyond the scope of this book. This much, however, may be said. The Church can only fulfil her function of being herself, the Body whereby Christ brings healing to the nations when each member of it is striving after wholeness of body, mind and soul. The prayer of faith has a great part to play in that, for each one of us.

2

THE HEALING GOD

THAT SICKNESS is, in some sense, the will of God is a view widely held. When some person dies of cancer after a long and painful illness, relatives may be heard to say "God's will be done." Commonly one may hear someone who is condemned for months or even years to live with a chronic complaint say, "Well, I must submit to God's will as cheerfully as I can."

The worse a complaint is, particularly if it is pronounced to be incurable, the more people are convinced that it can be nothing else but the will of God. A person may have influenza and get better, and it is by many generally accepted that the complaint and the recovery are both God's doing. If, however, the patient dies, then it is believed that the death is also His will, as if He had planned it that way from the very beginning.

In view of the total Scripture record, particularly that of the New Testament, it is strange that such a conception of God's character could be possible, for, from beginning to end God is clearly revealed in the Bible as a healing God. His whole purpose, we are told, is to bring all things to wholeness. The Divine plan is one of renewal, restoration, perfection.

It may be objected that here and there in the Old Testament we find phrases which suggest the writer believed that the miseries which affect a suffering humanity are a part of God's scheme of things. "Shall we receive good at the Lord's hand, and not evil?" If such an attitude can be read into certain passages, it is at best but a weak human interpretation of a state of affairs otherwise inexplicable to the writer, and in no way corresponds to the picture of God's character as generally depicted in Scripture. And in those formative days men were but as children in their knowledge of God. The Divine purpose and plan were gradually revealed until the character of God was most fully and finally made known in the Person of Jesus Christ.

In the book of the Revelation, and in the concepts best understood by his readers, St. John gives a clear picture of the end-product of God's purpose as he believed it, in the light of Jesus Christ's life and work. The contrast between this last book of the Bible and the first speaks its own lesson. In Genesis mankind is seen in sinful disorder, selfish, deceitful, murderous, struggling with painful labour to bring an unmastered creation under his dominion, and, in the process, at odds with God, the world and himself. In Revelation we see the final result of the redemptive process initiated by God Himself; man walking happily about a beautiful city, where there is no darkness, sin or sickness, and all is harmony and loveliness, and in the midst of it the Lamb, the Crucified and Risen Lord, Who in Himself has overcome evil and brought to humanity the possibility of perfection.

Even in Old Testament days, when some crude ideas of God were current, there were not wanting those who thought of Him as a healing God, one Whose purpose is to restore humanity to the perfection which had been lost by its own sinfulness. The writer of Psalm 103 specifically refers to God as one Who heals diseases as well as forgiving sin. The psalmist in Psalm 30 cries: "O Lord my God, I cried unto Thee, and Thou hast healed me."

*   *   *   *   *

There is no warrant in Scripture for believing that sickness is part of God's plan, any more than sin is. He can use it, and does. But He did not create it, nor does He of set purpose inflict it upon His people. He made all things *good*.

This is no place to discuss the origins of disease, nor the place of bacteria in the purpose of a beneficent Creator. All we are concerned to say here is that sickness is not the will of God. If you are ill, know that your sickness was not sent by Him. *His purpose is to heal*.

That purpose is made crystal clear by Jesus. He must have healed thousands of people, and He said He was doing God's *works*. God, He declared, is Love, and Love never hurts nor destroys, for, like all good qualities, Love is creative.

Indeed, God has made us in such a fashion that our whole being rebels at the very idea of being ill. Even though we may hold the mistaken notion that our sickness is God's will, we nevertheless go to any lengths to get well again! God's purpose is seen in this very fact—if in nothing else—that we all have the urge to throw off sickness. Even the little knife-wound in our finger shows, by the way in which the forces of the body set about healing it, that the life that is in us is working all the time towards wholeness.

Jesus declared that the Heavenly Father, Who made and loves the beauty and glory of the flowers, loves human beings a great deal more, and desires that they also should reveal, in their own measure, His loveliness, His glory, His beauty and His joy. That is why Jesus healed people; not in order to make them so grateful to Him that they would become His followers, but simply because they were ill, and God's will for them was that they should be well. If sickness were God's will, Jesus would never have healed a single soul or body. *Healing was so important a part of His mission that not only did He Himself heal, but He also commanded the Apostles, and through them His Church, to go out and heal the sick.*

All through His Ministry, and since then in the Church, Jesus has declared to us that God is a healing God. When, therefore, we come to our prayers, we come with the absolute conviction that our request for health is in accordance with God's will. We need come with no lingering doubts or fears, wondering if it is worth while. God's will for you, and me, is that we should be well and have fulness of health.

More than that, He is so set against disease that He is at this very moment working for our healing. "The Kingdom of God," said our Lord, "is among you." It is a present fact. God is present in us; His power is at work in us to restore and to heal. We do not need to appeal like beggars for Him to come and heal us. He is already doing that very thing. It is for us to accept in simple faith, and with deep thankfulness, the health that He is bringing to us. For He is a *healing God*.

*   *   *   *   *

To believe that God wills our sicknesses and diseases is actually one of the greatest barriers to the recovery of health, because it tends to encourage an attitude of acquiescence in a present ill-condition, the effect of which is to fasten the disease more firmly to us.

If we go about in darkness our eyes will become so used to it that darkness will be our light. But once we turn our faces to the light, not only shall we recognise the darkness for what it is, but we shall have taken the first step away from it. So too, once we have accepted that our sickness is contrary to God's will, and realised that He is actually at work to heal it, we shall have made the first, vital, move towards recovery.

The possibility of total healing, which is salvation, is good news indeed. It is, in fact, the Gospel, and Christ has brought it to us in His Own Person. This is not to say that those of us who have had diseases, or who die of diseases, have missed *salvation.* But it does mean that Christ's life is an open statement that sickness is no more a part of the Divine economy than sin is, and that it is God's declared will that we should come to wholeness at every level of our being. Jesus has assured us, and everything He did made it plain, that our Father is a healing God.

Go to your prayers with that absolute conviction, be sure of it, and rejoice in it.

3

HEALTH WITHIN

IT MAY BE ASKED, "If God is a healing God, how does He heal?" To answer this we must first pause and realise that without God, Who is the Creator, there could be no life at all, for He is the Author and Giver of it. Without the Life that God is, we should all be dead; creation would dissolve and there would be nothing. Everything that exists does so because God's life, God Himself, is in it. And because He is what He is, He is all the time creating, building, renewing. We cannot destroy life, for it goes on and on, in another direction.

Life is indestructible. It goes on creating, renewing, restoring, in a thousand mysterious ways. It is indestructible because God is indestructible. So long as it is His will that grass should grow, and birds sing and children be born, nothing that you or I can do will stop Him. We can twist the course of life, delay or hinder its work, mar and darken it, *but we cannot destroy it*.

This being so, it is obvious that wherever there is healing, wherever an agency is at work to restore sick personalities, the life of God is operating. God is, in fact, healing all the time by a multitude of means. He heals through an aspirin tablet, penicillin and other specifics. He heals by the surgeon's skill. He heals through the care of nurses, through the love of relatives and friends. He heals, too, by the laying-on of hands with prayer, and through the Sacraments, particularly in Holy Communion and anointing. And He heals by the prayer of faith.

In a word, the real healing power is God Himself, Who is within us. Everything else we do is helping to make the way clear for that life to do its work.

*   *   *   *   *

God is greater than His creation, but He is also in it. He is transcendent, that is, away above His world, but He is also immanent, that is, remaining in the midst of it.

The primitive people, whom we call animists, got hold of a portion of the truth. They believed that every creature had its appropriate spirit. There was a spirit of the river, of the tree, of the mountain, and so on. They worshipped these things, not because a spirit created them, but because a spirit lived in them.

The Egyptians worshipped the sun, because obviously without it there would be no life. And there was a god in the River Nile, because its water brought fertility without which life would be insupportable.

These are vague graspings at the truth that the great Lord of them all, Who created them and gave them life, is also keeping them alive, sustaining them, not only from without, but also from within.

The sun and rain bring life to the plant from without, in a sense, but inside of it are the tiny cells, perfectly adapted to their work, absorbing and distributing the sustenance. And the life of God is in them all, sun, rain and cells. It is invisible, intangible, it cannot be magnified, dissected or analysed. But there it is, and neither sun nor rain nor cells would be any use without it.

*   *   *   *   *

Jesus said, "The Kingdom of God is among you." It comes into being whenever we recognise the activity of God in creation. God's perfection lies about us and in us, God with all His eternal qualities of Love, Joy, Wisdom, Peace, and so on. With reference to ourselves, St. Paul puts it: "Know ye not that your bodies are temples of the Holy Spirit?" Speaking to the Athenians, who had temples and altars to all manner of gods, he said, "What therefore ye worship in ignorance, this set I forth unto you . . . He Himself giveth to all life and breath . . . for in Him we live and move and have our being." To the Corinthians, having in mind perhaps the heathen temples he saw on every hand in the cities he had visited, he declared, "Know ye not that *ye* are a temple of God, and that the Spirit of God dwelleth in *you*?" When we respond to Him, and act in awareness of His activity, the Kingdom is coming in us.

*   *   *   *   *

It is a wonder of the Gospel that it was in Jesus that the Spirit of God dwelt in all His fulness. He was indeed Immanuel, God with us. The life that He lived, by means of which He for ever destroyed all the power of evil, even through the grave and gate of death, becomes available to all men by faith in Him. True, it was already in the world, and in all men to some extent. Jesus is "the light which lighteth every man" (St. John 1: 9). But it is as we accept Him in faith that the light increases in us more and more, until we too manifest in our own souls and bodies the glorious conquest over evil which He won, both here and hereafter.

God, then, in all His goodness, is within us. This can only mean that the real source of health, the power to restore the faded tissues, the jaded spirit, lies within each one of us. Apart from it no amount of medicines, drugs or surgical skill will be of any use.

This is not to say we are free to despise the ministrations of the medical profession. Far from it. If all we have said so far is true, we should accept, and accept gladly, all that medical skill is prepared to offer us when we are ill. We are admonished in Scripture to *give place to the physician*.

If illness befalls us we do right to call in our doctor. Moreover, we should heed his advice, and do our best to co-operate with him. But it is no discredit to medical science to say that doctors themselves would agree it is not their skill or medicines or advice which actually heal. A surgeon once remarked, "I cannot heal. All I can do is to operate. Nature will do the healing." What he calls Nature is the life-giving Spirit of God, working within us.

*   *   *   *   *

Health is within. If that is so, it may be asked, "Why am I ill, then?" or, "Why do I not get better?"

We have to remember that God is not a magician. Nor is He a changeable God. Being the great authority behind and in all things, He works, as indeed any other lesser authority does, *by the rule of law*. If we are to draw from the life within its fullest blessings, we have to learn to co-operate with the laws of God, all of them, not just those we happen to like. Otherwise we cannot enjoy the privileges of the kingdom in which we live and move and have our being.

A government brings the rule of beneficent law to its subjects. If the law is broken then the people suffer. Just so, if we break God's laws, we cease to enjoy the fulness of His goodness, even while it is within our grasp.

*   *   *   *   *

God made all things "good." It was the entry of sin into human life that caused unhappiness and sickness. But the love that caused all creation cannot rest content with anything less than perfection, and so is constantly working towards it. "My Father worketh hitherto, and I work," said Jesus (St. John 5 : 17).

It is left to humanity to co-operate in that purpose. We are free to act as we will. And if evil enters into our life in any form, in sin or sickness or disease, it is because somewhere, somehow, God's laws have been broken either deliberately or in ignorance. Some of us may even be suffering in innocence through sin committed long ago.

But God does not set out to punish in a spirit of grim Divine displeasure. Humanity does not suffer for its sins, but by them. God is concerned to save, not to punish.

Viewed in this light, the Ten Commandments are seen to be, not a series of unfeeling prohibitions restricting our liberty, but the wise guidance of a kindly Father intent on protecting us from harm. It is as though God were saying, "I should not do this, if I were you; it will hurt you, so you had better keep off it." But He leaves it to us. Milton makes God say of Lucifer :

> "I made him just and right,
> Sufficient to have stood, though free to fall."

Nothing was wanting for perfection. Only sin spoiled it.

Sometimes we suffer by our own faults, sometimes by the faults of others, or, again, sometimes by reason of the accumulation of wrong-doing committed by the human race from time immemorial. But, whatever the precise ultimate cause of our sicknesses may be, one thing is clear. If health is within, if God's life is in us and round us, we shall do ourselves and others the greatest possible service *by obeying from this moment God's laws.*

B

There is much in the mind and life and environment of all humanity that acts as a serious barrier to recovery of health. We cannot pray successfully and hopefully for health until this is dealt with. To that subject we will turn in the next two chapters.

4

THE DISEASE CONSCIOUSNESS

IN HIS REPORT for 1952 the Medical Officer of Health for Hertfordshire stated that "too many children are already disease-conscious. Some way must be found of unobtrusively teaching children to live and think healthily as part of the ordinary preparation for adult life".

Other observers would go further and say that there is a great deal of disease-consciousness among adults, too, and that it is on the increase. How could it be otherwise, if adults have grown up in that consciousness since childhood?

If a child is disease-conscious it can only be due to the mental environment in which it lives. If its parents are always talking about the symptoms, causes and consequences of all manner of complaints, the child will absorb, and may go on to manifest, an atmosphere of anxiety and alarm whenever the presence of those symptoms become apparent. It is in just such an atmosphere that the diseases feared can most readily take hold.

If the child is constantly warned of the possible awful consequences of such-and-such an action, those consequences may begin to form a large part of its mental content. It will become aware of the power of those consequences, and not only will it go in constant fear of them (if only sub-conscious fear), but will also be always on the look-out for the symptoms, often imagining them to be there when they are not.

Parental anxiety for the good health of their little ones can sometimes be a boomerang, bringing back on the children the very things the parents are anxious about. To be forever filling the children's minds with thoughts of diseases, or even of minor complaints, may quite easily, though unconsciously, prepare the way for those complaints.

The awful power of suggestion over the mind, with its potential influence upon the body is well-exemplified in the well-known story *Fanny by Gaslight* in which an unscrupulous husband, by a series of mental tricks, persuaded his wife that she was going out of her mind. She began to act as though she were, till happily the deception was discovered.

But even if disease is never mentioned in a household, it is still possible for parents, and particularly mothers, to affect unconsciously the minds of their children with anxiety about health. The hidden effect of mind upon mind is more potent than many of us think.

The fearful, anxious, worrying thoughts of a parent, though covered with a cheery smile, can create an atmosphere which is drawn in by the children—especially very young ones—as easily as their lungs draw in breath, and just as naturally.

*   *   *   *   *

We think and talk far too much about disease. It becomes thereby as much a part of our mental furniture as the Government of the day or the daily chores. We live with it and it lives with us. Our pre-occupation and fear of it help to build up disease-consciousness.

Another powerful source of this disease-consciousness is due to the very progress of medical science itself. We have made great strides in the last fifty years in the isolation of disease germs, and the identification of many unknown diseases. We can now accurately name scores of complaints once ignorantly described in such general terms as "inflammation". As a result of our more exact knowledge and the widespread dissemination of medical facts in a multitude of popular papers, our minds have become increasingly stored with a great mass of medical information.

The Press, as well as shop-windows, abound with advertisements for specifics purporting to cure a thousand different ailments, detailed descriptions of which often accompany them. Much of this knowledge is superficial and ill-digested.

It is a fact that one of the most astonishing results of this pre-occupation with disease, combined with a skilfully managed patent-medicine advertising campaign, is that no less staggering a sum than forty million pounds is spent every year in the United Kingdom on drugs and patent-medicines of one kind or another. This is only the financial aspect of a disease-consciousness which beggars imagination.

It is probable, too, that the mass-examination of the public, which is now a regular feature of life, creates a morbid attitude of mind. The slightest suggestion of a disease can pave the way for the development of that disease.

*   *   *   *   *

In the opinion of some medical experts Britain has become the paradise of the chronic medicine-drinker, and the weak, anxious person who has grown up in the atmosphere which suggests that every little symptom may be the beginning of some serious trouble.

The institution of the National Health Service has helped to engrain this attitude still deeper. It has made the surgery queues longer and doctors are spending much of their working life re-assuring "patients" that there is very little the matter with them. But the "patients" continue to come, convinced that they might as well have the benefit of the counsel of a medical service for which they are paying. We are fast becoming a race of hypochondriacs.

The Health Service expresses a right principle: that the nation's health is a community concern. I believe it is doing a great work in many directions, but this ought not to obscure its proper object, which surely is the creation and maintaining of a healthy race at every level of its personality. The surest indication that it is fulfilling its true function will be not in the number of hospitals it opens, but the number it closes. It will always be hindered in this real aim so long as disease-consciousness persists amongst the people. This consciousness is one of the biggest factors preventing our doctors and specialists from getting on with their real work, that of creating healthy personalities.

*   *   *   *   *

It is remarkable how disease-consciousness is allowed to exist and spread through a race of people which in all other matters is noted for its stolid, sound common-sense. It is commonly said that the Englishman's conversation is mostly about the weather, especially bad weather! I wish it were true. But it is not. The commonest subject of conversation in England today is bad health.

Symptoms, diseases, complaints of every kind, are exhaustively discussed on every possible occasion, in trains, buses, queues, and, worst of all, in the very places where such talk does most harm, in doctors' waiting-rooms, sick-rooms and hospitals.

People seem to take a perverse pleasure in reporting their own and other people's illnesses to a most detailed degree. One detects a morbid resignation in the way someone describes his sufferings as being "hereditary", and how "Uncle Charles had it all his life". Or one can perceive the anxious fear, faintly concealed, of someone who is hearing of the progress, or otherwise, of another person who has got the same illness as himself.

Many a sick person's recovery has been retarded because some well-meaning visitor has spent an hour talking about illness. The one topic of conversation which ought never to be permitted in the sick-room is sickness itself. Yet more often than not it is the most popular subject. It goes on, adding more and more to the disease-consciousness which is the bane of our age.

Disease-consciousness lets loose and gives free play to all those emotions in which disease finds its strongest allies, fear and anxiety. Coupled with a lively imagination, or a sensitive nature, it can work much hidden harm. There is much truth in the statement that to fear anything is to tend to draw it towards us. Perhaps Job was speaking from experience when he cried:

The thing that I greatly feared is come upon me.

* * * * *

The report quoted at the beginning of this chapter suggested that some way ought to be found to teach people to "live and think healthily". The words ought to be the other way round. We cannot possibly live healthily without thinking in the same way. Healthy thinking comes first; healthy living follows. Nor can I see why the process must be unobtrusive. Right thinking must be positively obtruded upon the consciousness until it becomes an unconscious habit. Only when such thinking has become part and parcel of the unconscious mind will its work be unobtrusively carried out.

To combat the disease-consciousness, and indeed disease itself, requires first a healthy attitude of mind. "Whatsoever things are true . . . of good report . . . think on these things" (Phil. 4: 8). Before we can begin the business of becoming whole, Jesus said, we must *repent*, which simply means change your mind, change your way of thinking. If we are to pray for health, this attitude is indispensable. This question is discussed in a later chapter but, before we come to it, something must be said about the necessary preliminary to right thinking, namely, the destruction of wrong thinking.

5

GETTING RID OF THE REFUSE

EVERY HOUSEHOLD has a dustbin. In the course of a day a good deal of rubbish accumulates. None of it is of any further use and some of it is positively dangerous if not destroyed. So the contents are regularly removed from the house by people who know how to dispose of it. The bin itself is only a convenient incidental in the process; the important matter is *getting rid of the refuse*.

It is strange that many people do not apply the same common-sense to the contents of their mind. In the course of the day, and much more so in the course of a life, the mind accumulates refuse, material of no real value, some of which, if allowed to remain, will be dangerous to the house it stays in—the body. Nature has her own delicate mechanism for removing physical refuse automatically, but mental refuse is entirely under our own control. We should give it our serious attention.

I have suggested that a healthy mental life is a necessary condition of a healthy physical life. That is to say, we have got to be able to fill our minds with healthy thoughts. But we shall not serve any good purpose by trying to bring healthy thoughts into a mind already stocked with an unhealthy content. No one in his right senses would mix the food for his plate with the contents of the refuse-bin before dishing it up. Jesus led us to believe that before the room of a soul can be a fit habitation for the Spirit the dirt must first be removed; the room must be "swept and garnished". We need to try to recognise this dirt, this mental refuse, for what it is.

This mental refuse may be described in several categories, though I do not by any means claim that the classification which follows is a scientific one. Psychologists and psychiatrists would certainly list them differently. Nor do I take any account of such mental oddities as, for example, sadism, masochism and the like, though I feel certain that these conditions, too, may be dealt with by a proper process of healthy thinking.

*   *   *   *   *

The first category I would call "environment-thinking". All of us grow up in a certain mental environment. The mental attitudes and reactions which belong to that environment become a part of our own mental content automatically, and quite unconsciously.

To take a simple example, which has nothing to do with physical health as such: amongst some races at certain periods of history it was customary to be suspicious of a foreigner. He was to be distrusted implicitly, just because he was a foreigner. Amongst the Greeks the word for foreigner and enemy was the same. This attitude is hard to overcome, and it may still be found, even amongst modern civilised peoples.

Superstitions come into this category. People welcome a black cat, avoid ladders, abhor Friday the thirteenth for no other reason than that they have grown up with the notion that black cats are lucky, and that ladders and Friday the thirteenth are not. For centuries this attitude hindered the cause of medical science. Lepers, for instance, were always allowed to rot to death, because it was generally assumed that the disease was incurable and was due to the Hand of God. So everybody automatically shuddered in the presence of the horrible disease and nothing was done to relieve the sufferer.

So in these days cancer and tuberculosis are automatically feared, because they are so deadly, and in most cases thought of as "incurable". When certain physical symptoms appear this unconscious attitude towards them comes to the surface, and an automatic "fear-complex" comes into open operation, to lower the spirits and depress the mind still further.

We have all been surrounded from our youth by all kinds of fears and inhibitions and alarms, which have become ingrained in our unconscious thought, rushing to the surface in a given set of circumstances. In extreme cases these fears may easily cripple the very will to live.

We should always be ready to ask of any common assumption about this or that symptom "Why? How? What do I really *know* about it?" We have got to get rid of the accumulation of ill-informed, unreasoning attitudes to this or that circumstance, together with the fears and alarms they engender. They are refuse. We shall never step bravely out into the marvellous possibilities life offers us, in a spirit of joyous adventure, if we remain shackled by the unquestioned assumptions handed on from one generation to another, and which have no basis in fact or truth.

The attitude towards so-called "hereditary" diseases is also in this category. "I've got stomach trouble, you know, but it's in the family," someone says. "It's to be expected." So he imagines it to be quite "natural" that he has it, and will not expect to get better.

There is, too, the acquired consciousness, not necessarily based on fact, that there is always the risk of contracting a disease simply by being in an infected area, or near an infected person.

Get rid of this refuse. It does not necessarily follow that a man is an enemy because he is a foreigner. Because you have got soaked to the skin does not mean that you are bound to get pneumonia. If your mother and grandmother and great grandmother had stomach trouble, that is no good reason why you should have it. Let me go on to say that this gives you no right to be foolhardy, to go out and deliberately risk a soaking in the next rainstorm, or to thrust yourself unwarrantably into dangerous circumstances.

*   *   *   *   *

Another category of refuse may be termed "negative thinking". It is so called because it is a denial of the Truth, which is always positive and therefore creative. God is Truth, and all that is good is from Him, of Him, and in Him. Anything that contradicts the truth is denial, negation, and therefore destructive. Fear is a negative thought. So are anxiety and worry. They deny the truth that God loves us, that His love is part of the life in us, working in us for our good. The entry of fear into the mind means that we have let go, if only for a moment, of our trust in God.

"Perfect love," says St. John, "casteth out fear." That is to say, if love is allowed to permeate the mind, there is no room for fear; it cannot live in such a mind.

Anger, bitterness, hatred and resentment are negative thoughts of great destructive power. They deny the actuality of the qualities of God's life in us, of joy, peace, calmness, sweetness and contentment, all of them creative and sustaining qualities.

It is well-known that worry and mental strain are a prolific source of duodenal ulcers, that bitterness and resentment, bottled up and brooded on, perhaps for years, may well result in arthritis and kindred complaints. So get rid of the refuse.

*   *   *   *   *

Then, again, there is the category I call "inadequacy-thinking", all that line of thought which makes us feel we are not capable of grappling with a certain situation. A sense of frustration, feelings of inferiority, helpless self-contempt or self-loathing, all of them are damaging attitudes. In particular, the psychological and often physical consequences of a mental attitude which looks back to some event in which the person concerned actually *was* inadequate or frustrated may be specially noticeable.

These attitudes of inadequacy are a denial of the truth that the Divine love, the Divine care for us, is ever-present, able to snatch victory out of defeat, able to fit us perfectly for the tasks in life for which He has brought us into the world. They deny the truth that we are actually in the hands of God, that He is in fact bearing us up, making us all the time more and more adequate and superior to circumstances, if only we will not hinder Him, by persisting in seeing things with our own eyes, instead of with His.

Only by allowing "lively" thinking to become more and more the characteristic of our conscious and unconscious selves, in the sense in which the Bible uses that word, i.e. "life-giving", can we begin to manifest all the outward appearances of liveliness, of health.

It is no coincidence that the seven root sins are commonly called "deadly". Pride, envy, covetousness, anger, lust, are particularly so. They are as damaging to the consciousness of the person who entertains them as to the person to whom they are directed. They are, persisted in, deadly to the moral sense, and productive of deadliness to the physical frame. They carry the germs, so to speak, of mental and physical debility, and shut out the wholesome influence that the life-giving Spirit of God is always exerting in us. Persistent anger, even if suppressed, is not unconnected with apoplexy, for example, and that is probably one of its least harmful consequences. Viewed in this light it needs no great stretch of the imagination to see that these root sins may be deadly in another sense than that commonly accepted. So get rid of the refuse.

*   *   *   *   *

It is to be noted that when speaking of these things, negative thinking, environment-thinking and inadequacy-thinking, we are referring not so much to the contents of the conscious mind but to the accumulation of it all in a great hidden mass, fixed and fastened by the passage of time, and added to every time they are allowed conscious scope. This refuse lies in the unconscious mind, and it is at that level, therefore, that its damaging qualities have got to be counteracted. It is in our intelligent, persistent praying that the work of counter-action can best be done, both in health and sickness.

God—or if you like, Nature—did not make us to be diseased. We were made to be perfect, full of Love, Joy, Peace, Wisdom, Health, in body, mind and spirit. Nature works automatically, instinctively, by the rule of law. We must learn, since we are creatures of free-will, to co-operate with Nature, with God, both consciously and unconsciously. But because we are also rational beings, it must be conscious and deliberate in the first instance. Milton writes:

> "Accuse not Nature! She hath done her part;
> Do thou but thine. . . ."

So get rid of the refuse. Resolutely put away into the dust-bin as unwanted rubbish all destructive thinking, all harmful attitudes. They do not really belong to you. They are the debris of life. Then turn to the Truth, to the God Who waits to fill you with positive, creative life. Get the healthy attitude.

When we know and accept the Truth we shall be increasingly rid of all those hindering, hampering ways of thought which cause us to act and react in fashions that mar and destroy the image in which God made us—His own.

*   *   *   *   *

There is great danger in an over-readiness to relate specific physical conditions to mental states or emotions. Even if there be tolerable certainty that the contents of the mind have a definite bearing upon any particular complaint or disease, there must be a very careful handling of the case.

Over-enthusiasm in this matter, or eagerness to "prove a point", could have damaging results. Moreover, when we are examining the relationship between mental and spiritual conditions with bodily health we are entering into a very intimate, personal realm. We must be most careful. For this reason it is most difficult to establish facts, and a wise mind will hesitate before trying to reach conclusions, and will hesitate even more before daring to give advice which may well affect the whole future of this or that person.

No-one who has given this subject a moment's thought will be hasty to advertise "success-stories" in order to commend his theories. He will be wary of the temptation to parade cases to show that he is right. He will be unwilling to encourage the attitude of mind which Jesus deplored: "Except ye see signs and wonders, ye will not believe."

Nevertheless, from time to time, a case occurs which goes far to bear out the theory that mental and spiritual states lie at the root of certain physical disabilities. If only we can get at the cause, identify it and replace it, we have gone far to finding the cure.

*   *   *   *   *

One such case comes to my mind at once. There was a woman who was suffering from a mysterious eye-complaint. The eyes seemed to swell, and they grew red and very painful. I chanced to discover all this some six weeks after the trouble first appeared. The patient had got as far as the eye-specialists, who pronounced that the cause of the complaint was unknown, and that it would probably get worse rather than better.

Now I knew this person very well, and a great deal of her personal history. Her only remaining child had died three years before this, giving birth to a baby, which also died. A son had died several years before that. She was a very tender-hearted woman, a devoted mother, and happy with her husband as well as in all her other relationships. But the last blow, the loss of her daughter, was a great burden to her, and more than suspicion told me that she spent much time in tears.

I ventured to talk the whole matter over with her, and put it this way: "It seems to me that your eyes are telling you that they have really had just about enough of this, and that they cannot go on being treated in this way. You are hanging on so tenaciously to your grief that your sub-conscious mind has room for little else. This, combined with the fact that you are crying so frequently, is probably a major factor in the eye-complaint. You must get rid of your grief. Hand it over to God, Who is more than able to bear it. Let Him do with it what He will, but pass it over to Him. More than that, you must replace it with something else. Replace it with the knowledge that God is in fact giving you the very things which the loss of your daughter seems to have destroyed. Fill your mind with the truth that God can enable you to rise above all the grief, the sorrow, the sense of loss."

I was afraid that my friend might be offended by this approach, but on the contrary she agreed that these things might be so. And so I gave her a month's course of prayer and meditation appropriate to her need and she consented to use them in the way I suggested.

The eye-condition vanished within seven days. It recurred a few times in a much less troublesome form, but is now quite absent. I can imagine that some psychologists, and medical experts, may doubt that I am right when I say that I believe that in this instance there is some evidence of the theory that "the spirit of man is a major factor in all disease". But it seems clear to me that here was a case in which the major factor was very much in evidence, and where neither psychiatry nor clinical experience had the last word.

*   *   *   *   *

There was, also within my experience, the case of a catarrhal condition of long-standing which disappeared in the middle of a meditation. One could go on relating instances of this sort of thing. But enough has been said, I hope, to suggest to even the most cautious minds that more serious attention must be given to the relationship between spiritual and physical condition than is commonly thought necessary today.

We stand here on the threshold of a tremendous field of possibility, and I believe that a new era of hope lies before the human race if it is prepared to face the issues here honestly, indeed scientifically. "Getting rid of the refuse" has a vital part to play in the conquest of disease, and may yet prove more potent in the search for health than all the medicines in the world, valuable as they are.

6

THE HEALTHY ATTITUDE

NOT ONLY DID JESUS warn us of the need for sweeping and garnishing a room, but also of the danger of leaving it empty. "The last state of that man shall be worse than the first."

If, having determined that we will resolutely clear our minds of every kind of destructive thinking or attitude, we leave it at that, we shall be doing more harm than good. We shall be only repressing our thoughts, not banishing them. We are not to "resist" evil, Jesus said, but to overcome it with good. As we empty the room of our soul of the refuse, we must fill it with its proper furniture, the creative thoughts of God's Life. Unwholesome thoughts are to be replaced with wholesome ones. And we shall discover to our delight that it is not we ourselves, but the wholesome thoughts, which do the overcoming.

In an earlier chapter we saw that true health is primarily spiritual. It is in the wholesome or unwholesome consciousness, as the case might be, that health or sickness finds its real ground of expression. The cleansing and strengthening of the soul is the proper object of all healing prayer in the first instance. If it be true that the spirit of man is "a major factor in all illness"—and this has yet to be disproved—then prayer is of vital import in the healing process, because prayer is fundamental to spiritual development. Without personal prayer, the fulfilment of man's spiritual nature to the limits of its possibilities is beyond reach. Indeed, no real spiritual progress can be looked for if no place is allowed for prayer. It is a food for the soul, as are also the Sacraments.

Both prayer and Sacraments are means of communion with Divine Life. Sacraments, however, are primarily part of the corporate life of the Church, and have above all a corporate significance. Prayer is essentially a personal relationship. If this relationship is destroyed, or allowed to be undeveloped, the spiritual side of our nature is denied its proper sustenance, real damage is done to the personality, and true health, or "whole-th" is beyond our grasp.

*   *   *   *   *

Doctors are more and more realising that something more is needed in the creation of healthy personalities than drugs, medicine and scalpel. That something is the care of the soul.

The proper breathing-space of the soul is prayer, and it is largely by means of prayer that the consciousness of human beings can find that wholesomeness which is the ground and the guarantee of all health. There needs to be the right disposition, the healthy attitude, and God has made us in such a way that we are quite capable of achieving it. It is within our ability, not only to get rid of the refuse, but to feed the soul rightly, not only to sweep and garnish the room, but to furnish it well through prayer.

But prayer is not magic. Nothing is gained by the mere repetition of words. There must be understanding of their meaning, and—more importantly—a simple reliance upon, and an unquestioning trust in, the truths of which the words are an expression. Unless there be a right attitude of mind and heart, the repeating of a collection of pious phrases, however beautifully constructed, in the hope that they will "do some good", betrays a conception of prayer as intelligent as that which underlies the Chinese prayer-wheel. We shall not be heard "for our much speaking".

If we persist in regarding God as a kind of benevolent old magician to whom last-minute requests can be addressed, our prayer-life will never be satisfying. God is not a magician who can pull pre-fabricated answers out of a heavenly hat. Too often we regard Him as though He were. That is one of the reasons why we become increasingly despondent about our prayers, and perhaps lose our "faith" altogether.

*   *   *   *   *

Prayer is allowing ourselves to enter into God's Presence, and that Presence is not sitting on a golden throne in some undefined quarter of a celestial city. If we think that, we have got our spiritual geography wrong. The Presence is with us all the time. We have but to allow It room to move. "Behold, I stand at the door and knock," says Jesus. "If any man open We will come in unto him. . . ." Prayer begins once we allow ourselves to become aware of the Holy Spirit of God in us and around us.

God does not expect us to come to Him with urgent, anxious appeals for help, as though His blessings have to be dragged out of Him by the mere force of insistent words. He wants us to come in order to accept freely what He is already giving us. Thus it is more important in prayer to hear what He is saying to us, rather than casting about in our minds to find what we can say to make Him hear. "Speak, Lord, for Thy servant heareth." God has spoken, and is speaking all the time to us, if only we will give ourselves time to listen. We come to Him, then, not to demand, but to receive.

*   *   *   *   *

The right attitude, the healthy attitude, in which to do the listening is to realise that, no matter what may be wrong with us, in body, mind or soul, God is actually in us and round us, working for our healing. Even though appearances seem to contradict this, we must accept His word.

The healthy attitude is to allow the mind and heart to be filled with all those qualities of life, all those thoughts and emotions which are constructive and creative. The healthy attitude is the one which can be for ever giving thanks that what we are praying for (so long as it be according to God's law) is actually being given to us. "In God's Word will I rejoice: in the Lord's Word will I be given strength." (Psalm 56: 10.)

The daily prayers in the following pages are based upon this attitude. Therefore a large place is given to thanksgiving. It is, also, understood that those who use them are prepared to take God at His Own word, despite any apparent evidence to the contrary.

The healthy attitude accepts that God's healing grace is at work now, and is not reserved to be tapped by a few lucky ones; that the principles of life are in reality constructive, creative and restoring; that God's salvation, wrought in Christ, is in present operation. It believes that Jesus was speaking plain truth about God's law of life when He said, "Whatsoever things ye pray and ask for, believe that ye have received them, and ye shall have them."

Again, the healthy attitude is that which will allow the mind to dwell constantly upon the various aspects of that healing life which is God Himself. Day by day the mind will assure itself that the life it so much needs, with all its quality of goodness, is at work doing the will of God. It will meditate, now on God's joy, now on His peace, now on His strength. It will not attempt to think about these things, but just to look at them, until the truth of them becomes a part of the mental make-up more and more, day by day.

*   *   *   *   *

One way to do this is to let the Words of Life that God speaks be repeated in the mind at set times for five or ten minutes, two or three times a day. They can be recalled throughout the day if necessary, while going about the daily tasks, or while lying in bed, during an attack of pain or in times of restlessness.

In this way we can come to a deeper "knowledge" of God. True knowledge is a spiritual possession; it is knowledge, not of fact, but of truth, for the truth is ever greater and more abiding than fact. Facts can deceive, mislead and obscure; truth is abiding, unchanging. Meditation is a dwelling upon truth. And to experience the deep inner knowledge of truth will set us free. *For this reason, meditations ought to have a prominent place in prayer for healing.*

We should also allow our prayer-life to be comprehensive in its scope. The healthy attitude will reach out beyond ourselves to the needs of all men, interceding for them, especially for those who cannot pray for themselves. It will realise on their behalf that the healing life of God is for them and in them, too. Thinking of the needs of others will help to take our minds off our own troubles, and by allowing the thoughts of God's healing love to flow through us to them we shall ourselves experience the healing.

*   *   *   *   *

This process of getting rid of the mental rubbish, of wrong ways of thinking, and getting the healthy attitude, is summed up in the Divine words, "Repent, and believe the Gospel." The Greek word for repentance is *metanoia* and basically means "a change of mind", an alteration in attitude. So the evangelical command can be translated "change your mental attitude, and accept the Good News with your whole heart." Put away sinful thoughts, thoughts which miss the mark, and substitute the attitude which seeks goodness. Put away despair, and doubt and fear, and substitute hope, and confidence and trust. This is the way of life and health.

Confession of sin, and the change of heart and mind involved therein, has a healing value all its own, as have thanksgiving and intercession for others; a healing value, that is to say, upon persons who practise them, as well as on others for whom they pray.

Do not try to will yourself into health. The constant exercise of will-power involves an expenditure of your store of nervous energy which may well detract from your strength rather than increase it. Will power does not heal. God is the healer. Leave it to Him, and just use your will for determining that you are going to do that very thing.

*   *   *   *   *

I am aware that in all these pages I have said nothing that is new. If it were new, it probably would not be true, anyway. But what I have written seems to have been the experience of countless men and women. From earliest times men have believed that God, when He says, "I am the Lord that healeth thee" speaks truth, truth that has often been obscured almost to the point of obliteration. We can follow their lead and profit both ourselves and others.

Go then to your prayers. God is with you. His healing grace is for you. Seek healing in the depths of your soul as well as in your body. Cast out the rubbish and take up the positive, healthy attitude, which is determined to accept God at His word, and co-operate fully with Him. And He will bless you.

7

MEDITATION AND HOW TO USE IT

Eᴀᴄʜ ᴘᴀɢᴇ ᴏꜰ ᴘʀᴀʏᴇʀ in this volume ends with a *Silent Meditation*. Limitations of space forbid me from entering upon an exhaustive discussion of this subject. For a fuller treatment of it the reader is referred to the books mentioned in the Preface. But something must be said here about it in order to enable those who use this book to employ the daily meditations profitably.

*   *   *   *   *

Bᴇɢɪɴɴᴇʀs in the practice of meditation will find is helpful to learn about it from some experienced group which meets regularly. It will be found that this is a great strength to the individual, and it will go far to prevent the sense of disappointment which can afflict one who tries to learn alone.

But if such a group cannot be found, do not let that deter you from trying to enter into the silence. It should be possible for some minister of religion to give you guidance and to help you form a group of your own.

Those who have been practising meditation for years can profitably employ two or more different meditations in the course of a day. But beginners would, I think, be well advised not to attempt so much. It is doubtful whether they would be helped by trying to use two new meditations every day, as set out in Part II. It would probably be better if they used the one appointed for the First Day Morning every morning for a week, and so with the one suggested for the evening. For the next week, the ones set for the second day could be used, and so on.

In this way there would be more opportunity for the meditations to do their work, and for the consciousness to be renewed. But, of course, needs differ, and as the method becomes familiar, we will feel free to use this or that aspect of Truth in accordance with those needs.

*   *   *   *   *

The word "meditation" here means what is known as "contemplative meditation". To put it briefly, and at some risk of misunderstanding, contemplative meditation is a state of silent communion with God, a state in which we may draw from Him the Light and Life, the Health and Wholeness which He is. It is well to say that we are not necessarily in that state when we use the words. The words used, and the way they are used, are but a method by means of which we can arrive at the state of meditation. It may be a long time before true contemplation is reached. We must persevere.

The words used are an expression of truth about God, and our relationship with Him. They are based on God's own revelation of Himself in Holy Scripture. They bring to us a greater knowledge of God within ourselves. Rightly used, they will, in time, result in a perceptible manifestation, in mind and body, of the Goodness of which the words themselves are but signs or symbols.

But before the truth can thus be shown outwardly, it must first be deeply received. It must be willingly and faithfully accepted. Therefore the words should be used constantly and patiently. The *knowledge* of God we speak about is not the knowledge we acquire by reading books, or listening to lectures. True knowledge of God is a deep, inner awareness of Him, subconscious absorption of the Truth that He is, and is at work.

All great work is done "behind the scenes". The play that we see upon a stage is merely the final result of all that went before, the thought of the author, the planning of the sets, the work backstage. All of this is hidden. So it is in the spiritual life. Outward results can only happen when something is going on behind the scenes. We think of the tremendous acts of Jesus upon the stage of history, His marvellous teaching and wondrous works. But behind it all was the life of communion with the Father, the silences in the wilderness, the long nights of prayer.

His conquests were won first behind the scenes.

*   *   *   *   *

Now the stage of life, the platform on which we apprehend the happenings of time, is the mind with which we think and plan, apprehend and appreciate—the conscious mind. It takes note of everything. All the "characters" of life, the daily chores, the things we see and hear, the feelings engendered by every circumstance, come and go across the stage, and then pass behind. There they stay.

"Behind the scenes" in the language of human personality means the subconscious mind. It does not think. It records and reflects. It reacts automatically to set situations according to its present content. Its reactions can, and most often do, show themselves in some mal-adjustment of mind and body. It is there, deep in the subconscious, that *knowledge of God* must be absorbed. It is there that we can find true communion with God and become more and more aware of the whole life that God is. It is from there that the awareness can spread wider and wider, until our life can show forth outwardly God's wholeness, until His glory can *break out* in us.

The practice of meditation enables us to draw into the subconscious mind true feeling about God. We bide still in mind, allowing the words chosen to penetrate the deep, inner self. Without trying to think, we gradually become more and more aware of the Presence that the words symbolise.

It is then that we are approaching the unity with God in which there is a free flow between Him and us. It is at that level that the Divine Power can freely pass into us. From that point, if we are patient and faithful, we can begin, however slowly, to manifest in ourselves something of the truth of the words we have been using.

*   *   *   *   *

So then, in meditation, we are not seeking to learn something about God, but to become actually aware of Him, so that His Peace, His Joy and Wisdom and Strength, and all that He is, can spread through all our being.

Practice is necessary. To do it for a week, then give up because there are no "results" is a wrong attitude. It may be a very long time before we think we can perceive any effects. Nevertheless, each time we meditate, God does something in us, and if we persevere day after day, we shall eventually know the truth, and be free.

Do not try to think about the words. If the repetition of them should take your mind along other tracks, and you find yourself wondering what they mean, stop, and draw your mind gently back to the sentence. Repeat it in the mind over and over for a short while each day, even twice a day. At first, do this for only three or four minutes. The time can be lengthened as the method becomes familiar. If possible, use the same time and place. The value of this is that it enables you to discipline yourself. It may be hard at first to keep to your daily practice, especially if you try to push it in at odd times when you are not otherwise occupied!

There are other ways to pray, but meditation is a method too much overlooked. All prayer has as its object an abiding union with God. In any particular method, room must be found to allow God Himself to speak to us. Before He can do that, there must first be *awareness* of Him. In seeking that awareness, Contemplative Meditation has undoubted value.

But above all, there must be real *stillness*. The thoughts of the conscious mind must be stilled. There must be stillness in feeling, so that the Divine Feeling may take the place of all human emotion. There must be stillness of the will. Try to relax the body, so that it may not obtrude itself upon the consciousness. Get into that position in which you can be least aware of it.

Do not try to do anything. This method depends in no way upon our own effort. It seeks such unawareness of self as will permit the Divine energy to do its own work unhindered. It seeks such awareness of the Other that that Other may take possession of us wholly.

*　　　*　　　*　　　*　　　*

Those dictionaries which delve into original meanings of words tell us that the words "meditate" and "medicine" mean the same, i.e., to learn, as well as to heal. Another closely related root word means to "dwell upon". We will not be far wrong by claiming that by meditation we mean "healing by staying the mind". The Bible supports the claim, for there we read "Thou wilt keep him in perfect peace whose mind is stayed on Thee." And *peace* does not mean the absence of trouble; it means something much more positive, the active, harmonious working of body, mind and soul in every possible circumstance.

For Christians, that staying of the mind, that stillness in Divine Truth, means dwelling upon the Divine Being as He has been perfectly revealed to us in Jesus. Stay the mind, then. Be still, and know that He is God.

PART II

DAILY PRAYERS FOR HEALING
FOR A MONTH

O HEAVENLY FATHER, I thank Thee that Thou hast been with me all through the night, and I rejoice in Thy Presence with me now. Thine it is to uphold the whole universe, yet not for a moment hast Thou relaxed Thine attentiveness to my needs.

I would praise Thee, O Lord, with all my soul, and all that is within me would now praise Thy Holy Name for the love which has upheld me to the beginning of this new day. There is no darkness in Thee and Thy Light is still within me, whereby I might again see Thy glory, and fill another day with Thy praise. Glory be to Thee, O Lord. Amen.

☩

Dear Lord and Father, in my need I turn to Thee to pray that Thy Holy Spirit, Who is in me now, may increase in me more and more, filling every part of me until my soul and mind and body show forth the Light of Thy glory. I trust myself to Thy sufficiency, knowing that Thou art working in me for good. Enable me to go on trusting in Thy healing grace. Grant that nothing that may happen today may shake that trust, but help me in every event to cling surely to the knowledge that Thou art with me. I thank Thee, Father, that Thou hast heard me. I thank Thee, Jesus, that Thy Spirit of Life and Light is in me now to heal. Amen.

☩

Thy mercy is over all Thy works, O Lord, and I commit to Thy all-wise keeping the souls and bodies of —— and —— and —— knowing that Thou wouldst have them to be whole every whit. Help them to know this, and to trust themselves in child-like simplicity to Thee, that they may come out of darkness into light, out of sickness into health and give Thee the glory of it all. Amen.

✠

Silent Meditation

I am thy life.

✠

EVENING

Lord, I have much to be sorry for this night; for my fears, and doubts and restless anxiety; for my peevishness and selfish wants, my impatient and unkind thoughts and words; for all the cloud of self-concern. Forgive the shadows I have this day cast across Thy light. Yet it is only because that very light is still shining round me and in me that I know them to be shadows, for in spite of all my faults Thy love is still set upon me, lighting me with all the brightness of Heaven to reveal, not my shortcomings, but Thine Own infinite compassion for me, and Thou hast granted me Thy pardon in this very moment that I now thank Thee for it, in Jesus' Name. Amen.

✠

Thou hast lightened my darkness, O Lord, and by Thy great mercy Thou wilt surround me as with a shield from all the perils and dangers of this night, for the love of Christ my Healer. Amen.

Thank you, Holy Father, giver of life and health, for my betterness this past day; for the newness Thou hast been, and art even now, giving to me; for food and shelter; for friends' love and every healing ministration; for peace and rest and all the good things I have enjoyed this day; for this —— and this —— and this ——. Amen.

✠

Some there are, Father, who come to nightfall in pain; some in sorrow and anxiety; some with hopes dashed or fears before them. Help them to realise that Thou art with them, knowing their needs and working to meet them. Help them to lean on Thy present strength. I think specially of —— and —— and —— and see Thy healing grace in them. If I myself should have pain or any weakness now, enable me to give it to Thee, for Thou canst bear it and triumph over it, even as in Thy Son upon the Cross. So now will I go to rest, for it is Thou only who causest me to dwell in health. Amen.

✠

Silent Meditation

I am with you always.

SECOND DAY   *MORNING*

ONCE AGAIN, O loving Father, I lift up my heart to Thee in praise; praise for all Thy creation of loveliness, all Thy goodness around me, in me, to me, and praise above all for Thyself alone.

I rejoice and give thanks that Thou, who callest all the stars by name, hast called me, too, by name, and enabled me to call Thee Father, and to love Thee for it.

Thou hast opened my eyes for another day to see, both outwardly and inwardly, all the evidences of Thine intimate care for me, the beauty and order of all Thy made things around me, and the stirring of Thy Spirit within me, everything ministering to my deepest needs, everything conspiring, by Thine unchanging Wisdom, to renew in me Thine Own image of perfection, upon which Thy purpose is unwaveringly set. Though I myself may not feel it now, yet my wholeness, my salvation, is seen before Thine own eyes completed and unspoiled. I thank Thee, Father, I thank Thee, Jesus, I thank Thee, Holy Spirit. Amen.

✠

Lord, what will befall today I know not, nor can I be anxious for hours which are not yet come. But whatever the day may bring, it will bring always one thing more, Thyself. And all my prayer is that Thou wouldst take from my mind any thought of anxiety or fear. Help me today to co-operate confidently with each and every one who will come to further Thy healing work, to submit to my physicians, to be courteous to my nurses and cheery with my fellow-sufferers. Help me today in thought and word and deed to show forth Thy glory. Amen.

☩

Bless all sick, sad and sorry people with the sense of Thy real presence with them. Grant to all doctors and nurses, all workers for healing, to know that their skill, their sympathy and their compassion are all a part of Thy great design of Redemption, so that they may do their work with confidence and in hope. And I thank Thee for Thy wholesome love now at work in —— and —— and ——. Amen.

☩

Silent Meditation

Be still, and know that I am God within you, making you whole.

☩

EVENING

OUR FATHER, my Father, who art in Heaven, and yet in me, holy is Thy name, holy Thy purpose and Thy work. May Thy holiness, Thy wholeness, be more and more seen in me. Thy Kingdom is in Heaven and on earth; may it come with power and purpose in us all. May Thy will, for me and for all men, which is perfect wholeness, be done in us, in soul and mind and body.

I ask, as a child asks, not for tomorrow's needs but for those only of present concern; and I ask, as a child asks, for daily sustenance for soul and body, knowing that it will be given, is being provided now, my daily bread.

Wash out my wrong-doings; fill me with that knowledge of pardon which comes to those who forgive others, and enable me to be of a pardoning spirit. Bring me not into any trial too great for my soul, and keep me from thrusting myself, or being thrust into occasions of sin, but rather set me free from being a slave of any evil thing or thought.

All these things I ask with every confidence in Thine answer, for Thy rule is sure, Thy power unassailable, Thy glory undimmed forever. In them all do I trust and rejoice this night, and say, Be it so! Amen!

✠

The day has been full of Thy mercy and loving kindness, which have been ever of old. There have been many things to be thankful for; this —— and this —— and this ——, and others to which, perhaps, I have been blind. I thank Thee for them all, and I thank Thee, too, Father, for the increasing sense of Thy light and strength within me this day, for that sense of well-being which Thou dost pour over me as a flood. I thank Thee for my bed, and for the rest and sleep that will be mine tonight. Amen.

✠

I entrust to Thy safe-keeping, Thou Defender of the faithful, all my loved ones. . . . Amen.

✠

Silent Meditation

I am giving My peace even unto you.

THIRD DAY   *MORNING*

O THOU MAKER of all things, who didst create out of nothing, by Thy very love, all that is—I thank Thee for creating me. I thank Thee that Thou hast given me eyes to see Thy beauty, ears to hear Thee speaking to me, a mind to know Thee and a heart to love Thee.

O Thou Redeemer of all men, by whom the worlds were made, and who in flesh hast purged and uplifted our human state, to make it into the likeness of Thine own divine order, I rejoice that this Thy saving grace is come to me also. I thank Thee that in the laying down of Thy life Thou hast raised mine up to the fullness for which the Father made it.

O Thou Spirit of Life, who didst move over the face of the dark and formless deep, to bring light and order, shape and beauty, I praise Thee that Thou art still about that same divine work in me, so that the hidden beauty of health might be made manifest, that disorder and disharmony of mind and body might be turned into the perfect and wholesome working of every part of me. I thank Thee for Thy life moving in me, that I may reveal in my person the glory of the Blessed Trinity, Maker, Saviour, Life-giver. Amen.

✠

I will go forth today in Thy strength, Lord God. Enable me all this day to think of, and seek for, Thy Rightness, and by Thy Spirit make that Rightness to come to pass in me, in thought, word and deed. Amen.

Silent Meditation

My love is now making you whole.

☩

EVENING

BLESSED JESUS, Who didst come to destroy in Thine own Person the works of the evil one, destroy now in me all the signs of evil, and renew in me the Spirit of Life:

Destroy my pride and give me lowliness;
Destroy my hate and give me love;
Destroy my sadness and give me joy;
Destroy my turmoil and give me peace;
Destroy my fretfulness and give me patience;
Destroy my unkindness and give me a feeling heart;
Destroy my ugly thoughts and give me gentle goodness;
Destroy my fear and give me trustfulness;
Destroy my self-assertion and make me strong for others;
Destroy my self-indulgence and give me self-control.

I thank Thee, Jesus, that Thy Holy Spirit is now at work to bring to light in me His holy fruits. May I put nothing in His way. Amen.

☩

The day is gone beyond recall; its deeds cannot be undone nor its words denied. I am sorry for such of its evil as was due to me, and ask Thy pardon, O understanding Father, for Christ's sake. Amen.

And as I leave the day behind, and try to forget my failures, yet would I not forget Thy successes; Thy love which has overcome evil, Thy constant care which has clothed and fed me, all the ways by which Thy guiding Spirit has this day brought goodness to light in multitudes of men and women in every place. I would remember all the signs of Thy conquering grace everywhere, and of which Thou hast granted even me a share. Praise be to Thee, O Lord. Amen.

✠

I turn now to grateful sleep, content to rest in Thy safe-keeping. Amen.

✠

Silent Meditation

Thou art keeping me in perfect peace.

FOURTH DAY   *MORNING*

O LORD, now I open my eyes to look, not only on another day, but also on Thee, who art my Strength and Stay. Thou hast taught us to come to Thy throne of grace with our petitions boldly, not as slaves in doubtful anxiousness, but as children, confident of our Father's love. So now I come, to lay before Thee my present needs, not because Thou art blind to them, but because I need to know the comfort of speaking with my own Father of those things which are near to Thy heart as well as to mine.

Come, then, in Thy Spirit of life-giving love, and fill me more and more with Thy Life; let it surge through me silently and surely, till every part of my being is shining with its glory and quick with its grace. Move in me now—see, I open the doors of my heart that it might be so—and bring to my heart and lungs, and all my organs, the freshness of renewal; bring new vigour to all my muscles; calmness to each and every nerve; vitality and power to all my cells and tissues. Flood deeply into my mind and soul, that they may glow with Thy truth and wisdom.

So do these things, Thou Lord of Life, that I might wholly praise Thee in the power of my soul, in the thoughts of my mind and in the deeds of my body.

And I thank Thee, Father of all wholeness, that Thou art enabling me now, not only to pray for these things, but also to see them in very truth accomplished. I thank Thee, Lord, that Thou art doing these things that I have prayed for. Keep me ever with a grateful heart for this Thy goodness. Amen.

Silent Meditation

I am the Lord that healeth thee.

✠

EVENING

Though we be sick, Lord, Thou art still whole;
Though we be weak, Thou still art strong;
Though we be out of harmony in this present time,
   Thou still art perfect peace for ever;
Though we be anxious of our condition, and doubtful of our
   future state, Thy will shall still be done.

And when, O Lord, my spirit's eye is dim and my grasp on
Thee falls slack, I turn again to know the Truth, that Thou
art in me, and I may be in Thee. So shall Thy will be done
in me; Thy peace shed o'er me; Thy strength uphold me and
Thy wholeness heal me. By Thy Son's command I claim Thy
love and know that it is mine, and in its sureness lay me down
to rest, at peace with all the world, because I am at peace with
Thee. Amen.

I commend to Thy mercy all who are awake this night:

   doctors tending the sick;
   nurses ministering to their wants;
   police and firemen guarding us;
   night-watchmen and those who drive on road and rail;
   men working on the sea, in the sky, and struggling with
   wind and wave;
   those who toss and turn in pain or restlessness;
   and those who only watch and wait.

May they know and welcome Thy sustaining love, doing what they must as work for Thee, and use them, Lord, in Thy great design for all men's good. Amen.

In Thee will I rest, now, O Lord, for the night is also Thine. Amen.

✠

Silent Meditation

Be still, and know that I am the Eternal Spirit of Health within you.

FIFTH DAY   MORNING

BLESSED FATHER, Thy Son Jesus Christ has said: *Be not afraid.*

Help me now to believe these words. Let me not look forward into this day with any anxiety or fear for what might befall me, but only let me thank Thee for Thine unfailing Presence, in me and around me.

Thy Son has said: *Be of good cheer.*

Help me now to mark all the signs of Thy goodness and love; to remember that He overcame all the evil in the world, and to rejoice therein. Help me to have a thankful heart for His triumphant love.

Thy Son has said: *Be not anxious for the morrow.*

Help me now to set about this day's business cheerfully and in hope. Help me to do my duties diligently, and not to worry about those that are not yet before me, and to leave all my tomorrows in Thy hand.

Thy son has said: *Love one another.*

Let this be my chiefest business today, and help me to do it ungrudgingly, for His sake. Amen.

☩

Give me grace, O Present Lord, to do all I can today to help those whose duty and joy it is to help me; my physicians and nurses, if I should need them, my loved ones and the friends who visit me. Enable me to think, not on my weakness, whether of soul or body, but on Thy grace which is healing me, and help me to know that, even when I forget Thee, Thy Love is still restoring me, for Christ's sake. Amen.

☩

Open the eyes, O Lord, of all who at this moment are experiencing pain, fear or sorrow of heart, or whose spirits are low, to know that they are not alone. Set them free from their anxious prisons to find peace and comfort in Thee. Amen.

☩

Silent Meditation

I will put My spirit in you,
and you shall live.

☩

EVENING

EVERLASTING FATHER of Wisdom and Light, Thou that art the hope of all the ends of the earth; even my hope is in Thee. Thy love has never left me all this day now nearly gone. Still, in spite of all my sins and faults, in spite of all my failings and negligence, that great love, made plain to us in Jesus Christ, is fixed on me, even me, this single soul among all the multitudes of the earth. Forgive my undeservings of that love. Accept for Thy glory such good things as I have had the grace to do, and take my humble thanks for all Thy gifts this day. Amen.

Lord, I have called unto Thee and Thou hast heard me. I have asked for Thy healing grace, and Thou hast not refused me. Even now I know the light of Thy Holy Spirit is within me to renew and rebuild. Thanks be unto Thee, O Lord. Amen.

✠

Praise be to Thee, Loving Lord, for Thyself, and for Thy marvellous great kindness shown to me in my need. Thanks be unto Thee for those who today have helped me and done me good . . .; for those who came to see me; for gifts received and books to read; for the loveliness of music and the beauty of art; for those who have recovered from their sickness and gone away made whole; for all that has reminded me of Thy great glory, and for the joy in everything that Thou hast put into my heart. Glory be to Thee, O Lord Most High. Amen.

✠

Silent Meditation

Thou art My servant, in whom
My Glory shall break out.

SIXTH DAY   MORNING

Lᴏʀᴅ of all life, Who didst command "Let there be light",
    and there was light, let me now by the light of Thy
    Spirit see Thy living glory in all created things, Thou
who art in all things yet not contained by them.

Praise to Thee for Thy glory in the everlasting hills that
stand unmoved except by Thy desire;
Praise to Thee for Thy glory in the sun and moon and all
the stars that shout together for joy;
Praise to Thee for Thy glory in the singing seas and little
lakes;
Praise to Thee for summer's smiling flowers and autumn's
falling leaves;
Praise to Thee for the friendly beasts and the birds that cry
their laughing canticles;
Praise to Thee for growing grass and trembling tree;
Praise for the art and skill of men in mirrors of Thine own
beauty;

Help me myself to be an image of Thy glory. Amen.

☩

I pray today for all who write, in books or papers, that they
    may write nothing but what is true;
For all who carve or paint or draw, that their work may be
good to look upon;
For all who speak, that their words may be wise;
For all who rule, that their guiding may be right;
For all who try a cause, that their decisions may be just;
For all who labour by hand or head, that their work may be
satisfying to themselves, and good for all.

For all men everywhere, that they may desire the good and
deny the evil;
Until, O Lord, the earth is filled with Thy glory as the waters
cover the sea. Amen.

☩

Here I am, Father, alive with Thy sustaining power for yet
another day, and as I dedicate myself to Thee, and renew
my trust in Thy goodness, so may I this day know within
myself the working of Thy grace, and manifest in my doings
the beauty of Thy nature, for Christ's sake. Amen.

☩

Silent Meditation

*Son, thou art ever with Me; all
that I have is thine.*

☩

EVENING

O GOD, Whose never-failing providence hath ordered,
and doth order, all things, I beseech Thee to take
away from me all hurtful things, and, as Thou dost
give me the things which are good for me, so help me to
continue in them always. Amen.

☩

Father, from Whom do come all things that are wholesome
and holy, all things that are good, all things that are true
and right, give me Thy servant to open my heart to Thine
incoming peace, so that I may be ever determined to do Thy

will. And as I know that Thou art defending me from all fear, so I shall pass all my days in rest of heart and mind, and in quietness of spirit. Amen.

✠

From fear of want and trouble,
From fear of poverty and insecurity,

I rest, O Lord, in Thee;

From fear of sickness and disease,
From fear of pain and suffering,

I rest, O Lord, in Thee;

From fear of weakness and of falling,
From fear of helplessness and inadequacy,

I rest, O Lord, in Thee;

From fear of present darkness and all the things that worry me,
From fear of that which is unknown,

I rest, O Lord, in Thee;

For Thou hast delivered me out of all my fear. Amen.

✠

Silent Meditation

*Be still, and know that I am the
Eternal Spirit of Peace within you.*

O BLESSED JESUS, my Master and my Friend, teach me
Thy way of living;

Teach me to know, deeply in my inmost being that God my
Father is sustaining me;

Teach me to know, without shadow of doubt, that His love
is fixed on me, and faileth not;

Teach me that that great love is healing me, and renewing
every corner of my being;

Teach me, Good Master, that my Heavenly Father knows
all my needs, and is fulfilling them now;

Teach me that my body is an abiding-place of Thy Holy
Spirit, and that His Light is shining in me more and more
unto the day of my perfecting;

Teach me, Good Lord, that I am ever in Thee, and Thou
in me, and that I shall lack no manner of thing that is good.

And teach me, Thou Chief of Ministers, to minister also myself
as far as in me lies, to the wants of other folk round me, and
to do it willingly and cheerfully, that seeing Thee in them,
I may thus minister unto Thee. Amen.

✠

Thanks be unto Thee, Heavenly Father, for that Thy Son
Jesus Christ has brought unto us the true knowledge of Thee
and a certain hope of Thy goodness; help me, not only to
acknowledge this truth, but so to trust in it with my whole
heart and soul, that I may share in Thy heavenly treasures,
both here and hereafter, for His dear Name's sake. Amen.

✠

Behold, O God, Thou art in all things, see, Thou never left
Thy hands from Thy works, nor never shall, without end.

See, Thou art leading all things to the end Thou didst ordain it to, from without beginning, by the same might, wisdom and love, that Thou madest it with. How should anything be amiss? So, Lord, will I trust Thee this day. Amen. (From Julian of Norwich.)

✠

Silent Meditation

I am the Christ, the Son of the Living God, within thee. By thy desire I am come to regenerate thy consciousness.

✠

EVENING

O GOD, all-knowing and all-wise, on this day Thou didst rest from all that Thou didst make. Thou didst bring it all forth from the womb of Thy love, and didst see that it was all very good, and still Thou hast determined that it shall become what in truth it is, for Thou dost never cease invisibly to work.

Forgive, O Compassionate Creator, the sin and ignorance, the blindness and stupidity of us Thy creatures, which have drawn a veil across Thy glory, that glory which in spite of all we do breaks yet forth in glimpses of Thy never-failing light and love.

Forgive me my own transgressings, and make the light of Christ to grow in me in splendour, until Thou canst see in me the unsullied likeness of His perfection. Rest not, O Lord, from Thy creative work in me, and help me to rejoice in Thy restoring love. Amen.

As earthly light now fades, I turn to Thee, Good Lord, my heavenly light. Once more I bow my soul in reverence and awe of Thee, which is the beginning of knowledge. Keep me, Father, in this holy fear, by which alone I may begin truly to experience Thy ceaseless Presence. Let Thy light increase in me until its radiance overcomes every failing, fault and fear. So shall I know Thine unspeakable Peace, and unafraid rest in Thy Strength. Amen.

In peace and trust I commend to Thee

> *Those who will pass the night in pain;*
> *Those who will lie awake unrestful;*
> *Those who face a crisis;*
> *Those who have suffered a shock;*
> *Those who watch by the sick;*
> *Those who will not wake on this earth.*

And for those, dear Lord, who at this moment contemplate some evil thing, I pray Thy love and mercy, for Christ's sake. Amen.

Silent Meditation

That I may know the healing power of
Thy Strength and Peace within me.

EIGHTH DAY   MORNING

ETERNAL FATHER, Whose Blessed Son has promised that it is Thy good pleasure to give us the Kingdom, praise be to Thy Holy Name for the love which day by day is bringing this to pass.

Praise to Thee for the knowledge of the Kingdom revealed in Jesus;
Praise for its beauty made plain in all His words and deeds;
Praise for His sacrifice of love which has declared its power and triumph;
Praise for the Kingdom of Christ which has broken the power of evil;
Praise that the gates of hell cannot prevail against it;
Praise that even I may enter therein.

Fill Thou me ever with Thy praise, my God and King! Amen.

✠

Almighty Father, King of Heaven, give me grace each day to seek, above all other things, Thy Kingdom; to seek it by patience and perseverance, by labour and love, by sacrifice and, if need be, by suffering; to seek it in peace and in turmoil, in sickness and in health, in temptations and in persecutions, in times of calm and times of tribulation, in times of danger and in times of safety; to seek it in the world, in the Church and in myself, for the sake of Him, the King of Love, even Christ our Lord. Amen.

Thou, dear Christ, art my loving King, and Thy goodness to me fails not; I shall want for no thing that this day needs, for I am Thine and Thou art mine, for ever. Amen.

✠

Silent Meditation

*Infinite Spirit of Love that dwells
within, I put my trust in Thee.*

✠

EVENING

I THANK THEE, Father, for this, another day that Thou hast given me; for its joys and pleasures; for its gifts and graces; for the food it has provided, and the friends it has brought near; for the work I have been able to do, and for the periods of rest; for the multitude of little things that make it big with Thy mercy.

And I thank Thee even for anything, this day of sadness and sorrow, of difficulty or hardship, of setback or delay, of disappointment or frustration; for they have taught me yet again of my need of Thee, and of Thy readiness to bear me up. I thank Thee, Father, for bearing me through the day in the adequacy of Thy strength. Help me now to rest in that same, all-availing power, and to compose myself for restful sleep, knowing that Thou art preserving me to fulfil the end for which Thou didst in the beginning create me. Amen.

I pray tonight for any who are desperately sick in mind, body or soul, and who are losing hope of recovery and restoration, or who despair even of Thy very love, especially —— and ——; enable them to come to a sure knowledge that Thou art Creative Spirit within them, keeping them, and taking away their fear. Help them to see with the eyes of faith that Thou knowest, and art protecting and healing them, even now. Amen.

Glory to Thee, my God, this night,
For all the blessings of the light;
Thou keepest me, O King of Kings,
Beneath Thine Own almighty wings.
                                        Amen.

Silent Meditation

*Thy consciousness shall be healed,
inspired, uplifted, by the incoming
of My Love.*

NINTH DAY   *MORNING*

As NOW, my God, I open my eyes to look on Thee in humble adoration, before ever I set my mind on the day before me, with its duties and demands, I rejoice and give thanks for the knowledge that countless others of every race and tongue are also lifting up holy hands to praise Thee their Maker. I pray in Christian fellowship with them, and for them.

Thanks be to Thee for thy holy Church in all the world, proclaiming Thy Kingdom;
For the witness of its people down the years;
For the fellowship of its saints surrounding me;
For the teaching of its doctors and the example of its martyrs;
For the courage of its prophets and the service of its shepherds;
For all the guidance and strength it has given to the onward march of the human race;
For its preaching of the Good News, and the Sacraments of Grace it brings;
For my share in its life, and all the richness of its inheritance I am privileged to enjoy, accept my humble thanks, Good Lord.

O Loving Father, Whose Blessed Son Jesus Christ is the tree of life for the healing of the nations, give Thy Church that mind and heart which was in Him, to go forth with joyful confidence into all the world, to bring to every living soul the great Gospel of Thy Healing Love, in the power of the Spirit, Who proceeds from Thee in Him, that all human life might be made whole.

May the coming of the Gospel heal the disputes in men's daily occupation; heal their broken marriages and their frenzied quarrels; may it draw together their opposing views, and make whole their fears and suspicions of each other. May it heal their poisoned thoughts and emotions. By the Light of Thy Gospel make the nations heart-whole. Amen.

☩

Silent Meditation

Be still, and know that I within thee am Life; I will have health, not disease.

☩

EVENING

HOLY FATHER, Holy Jesus, Holy Spirit, I humbly acknowledge Thy Divine Presence within me, imparting to me all the riches of Thy Perfect Life. Day by day I am drawing on Thy Goodness; day by day I am living and moving and having my being in Thee. All the benefits of Thy wholesome strength that I am receiving I have myself done nothing to deserve, for there has been no good thing in me that Thou hast not Thyself already given me of Thine own free Love.

Wherefore, Eternal Holy One, in Whom alone is my life, remove from me, from my mind and heart, from my deepmost consciousness, every trace of that which leads to death, everything that would hinder the life Thou givest:

Remove my pride, and give me humility;
Remove my envy and give me generosity;
Remove my covetousness and give me liberality;
Remove intemperate ways, and give me moderation in all things;
Remove lust, and control my every desire;
Remove my anger and give me gentle patience;
Remove my sloth, and grant me the active, enthusiastic spirit;

Forgive me where I have gone amiss today. Enable me to receive in faith and hope the pardon Thou hast promised in love, and strengthen me yet more in the service of Thy Kingdom. Amen.

✠

Bless, Thou Light of men, all those who strive for good, and feel inadequate;
Those who feel they make no spiritual progress;
Those who feel too sinful to turn to Thee again;
Those who despair of ever living well;
Those who are overwhelmed by sense of sin;
Those who have given up hope of goodness in themselves;
Those who are losing, or who have lost, their faith in men, in life, or in Thee.
Help them to know the Truth, and to learn to hope again. Amen.

✠

Silent Meditation

Acquaint thyself with Me, and be at peace.

TENTH DAY   *MORNING*

TEACH ME, Father, to pray for more faith to trust in Thy promises, more faith to trust my whole self to Thee, more faith to leave everything utterly to Thee. Help me to pray that I may act towards Thee as a child, completely forgetting everything that is past, and looking forward with deep expectancy to the healing that Thou art willing to bring forth in me.

Help me to cease to hug my grievings and troubles to myself and to throw them into the furnace of Thy purging and healing Love; then shall I know, with the knowing of experience, Thy wholeness, Thine abundant Life. Amen.

☨

Teach me, Father, to pray for more love in my heart; more love for Thee and for my fellow-men; for love that is deep and understanding and generous; love that is warm and full and true; love that seeks no return, but only seeks to love. Teach me to lose myself in love, that I may find myself in Thee. Teach me, Lord, to love, and to love, and yet again to love. Amen.

☨

Good Lord, yesterday is gone, tomorrow not yet come. This is today and Thou art in it, for Thou art the "I Am", the One that Is, and Thou art true to Thyself, yesterday, today and tomorrow. What Thou hast been, Thou wilt be; what Thou wilt be, Thou art. Therefore I do not need to wait until tomorrow to know Thy saving health.

If my body aches, or breathing is hard, or nerves are strained, I do not need to wait and wonder if Thou wilt come to help me, for Thou hast said "Now is the day of salvation." So now I lean on that promise; now I surrender my troubles to Thee; now I accept Thy salvation.

Thy promises are timeless, and how should I be excluded from them? Thy Word is not an empty thing. It will come to pass. I leave all to Thee, and will do all I can to help. Here I am; I am Thine; Thou art with me and I am at peace. Amen.

✠

Silent Meditation

I would know the strengthening power
of Thy healing Love within me.

✠

EVENING

FATHER OF ALL goodness, Whose marvellous Love, Uncreated and Eternal, cannot tolerate anything that is evil, I thank Thee that Thou art ever ready to burn away all the dross that makes me unworthy of Thee. I thank Thee that Thy forgiveness is a reality, and means "never to be able to remember again."

Give me grace now to relinquish all that is past, to let it float for ever away and sink in the ocean of Thy Love, never to be seen more. Help me, as I acknowledge my sins, this —— and this —— and this ——, to acknowledge also that Thou hast pardoned them.

But more still, Good Lord, help me not to torture myself with my failures and faults, but to look them down, to face them with Thy Love, and to say to myself, "You are forgiven", to acknowledge to myself that I am clean in Thee, clean with the cleanness of Thy pure Heart, and whole with the health of Thy Salvation. Amen.

✠

Lord, I am grateful for what Thou hast done in me this day, grateful that Thine hand is laid upon me for good, grateful that the Risen life of the Risen Saviour is in very truth within me now, quickening every fibre of my being, making me alive with the Life Eternal, alive with joy and gladness, alive with strength and peace, alive with health, deep, real, strong and sure. I am grateful for the power of the Invisible Spirit, stirring silently and mightily within me, grateful for the vital renewal given me this day.

Teach me, O Lord, an ever-increasing gratitude for Thy never-ceasing healing power within me, and help me to seek the reality of Thy health not only in my body, but deep also in my soul. Help me to seek first for health there, that I might the better enjoy and use for Thy glory the strength of body that is Thy will for me. Amen.

✠

Silent Meditation

I am the Eternal Spirit within you, giving you the strengthening and re-creating power of My Life.

ELEVENTH DAY   *MORNING*

THOU KNOWEST, my All-wise Father, the weakness of my
heart, how so easily I become a prey to fear in every
little adverse circumstance, how my soul seems to shrink
and my resistance to fall limp when some crisis comes upon
me. Thou knowest how readily I am persuaded to run like a
frightened rabbit back into the dark burrows of my anxious
watchfulness, there to be blind to the great, fresh world of
Thy Life about me.

Thou knowest all this, and I know it. But more I know, that
I can never escape Thy Love, so that if I go down into hell,
Thou art there also. There is no darkness that can hide Thee,
nor sin that can shadow Thee. Thy hand is over all Thy works,
and over me. No matter, then, what my flesh should feel, or
my outward sense persuade, I know with inner knowing that
Thou art in me, enabling me to look my disabilities in the face,
and to say to them, "The Lord rebukes you".

So now I turn once more to look at Thy Light, and the
shadows fall unseen behind me. Thou hast promised to put
Thy Spirit in me that I might live. I believe it; I trust it; I
know it. I thank Thee, Lord, for Thy Life and Light and
Love, in me now. I am content. Amen.

✠

Praise to Thee, Saving Lord, for the Church everywhere,
Thy Resurrection Body here on earth. Help it to be faithful to Thee, and to show forth the light of Thy healing grace
among the nations. May all its members be conscious of the
Life that is in them, that they may be more and more effec-
tive channels of it, for Thine Own Name's sake. Amen.

Silent Meditation

My perfecting Love is within
you, casting out every fear.

☩

EVENING

FATHER OF ALL mercies, Thou hast taught us that we in Christ are dwelling-places of the Spirit of Life. Let Thy Spirit break forth in me now, to reveal Thy Glory in my soul, in my mind and in my body. Let Him do His silent work of healing in any physical weakness that I may have, for that is Thy Will. Let Him also heal the weaknesses of my mind and soul.

Come, Holy Spirit, and heal now my understanding; heal the deepest, hidden realm of self; heal now what only Thou canst heal. Heal the dark, unconscious cellars of my mind—too full of the hurts of all my life; heal my memory and my cherished grudges and resentments; heal my treasured griefs and sorrows; heal my desires and my ambitions; heal all my motives and my ignorant graspings after things that are not good for me; heal the wounds of disappointment and the palsies of frustration. Gently release all the chains that bind me, and bring me into the freedom of Thy perfect sufficiency. So shall I be glad all the days of my life. Amen.

☩

Lord, I would be still for a while this night, and pause in the midst of this rushing, troublous life, and stay my mind on Thee. I would be still, and know that it is indeed true that Thy Peace, Thy Joy, Thy Love, Thy Strength, are in me now. I would be still, and realise the sureness of Thy hold upon me and Thy Power in me.

I would be still and know all this. . . .

Have pity on my faltering faith, and help me to be more and more conscious of Thy life-giving Presence. And what I ask for myself I ask for all men, and especially for my loved ones, wherever they may be. . . . Amen.

☩

Silent Meditation

I will fill thy mind with knowledge of Me, and keep thee in My Perfect Peace.

D

TWELFTH DAY　　　　　　　　　　　　　*MORNING*

FATHER, it is another day to me, but to Thee still the same timeless moment of Thy vigilant Love. Here I am; and here art Thou. If I speak with Thee a thousand years, yet could I not exhaust the tale of this one thing, Thy Love. So I will not speak much, but, rather, listen to Thy eternal voice saying,

> *Be still, and know that I am God within you;*
> *I have never left you.*

And with that assurance, Lord, I face the day gladly; in the strength of it I will go forth.

I look forward this day to a renewal of my health, to increased strength, to re-creation of bone and cell and tissue. Increase in me that sense of expectancy, that I may grasp Thee with faith and not with anxiety, and let my hold on Thy promises be firm till evening comes again, and help me to be more and more deeply aware of Thy fulness within me, till I shall know even as I am known. Amen.

✠

GOOD Master Jesus, I thank Thee for, and ask Thy continued blessing upon, all people whose work and joy it will be today to heal, by whatsoever means:

> *For doctors who advise and prescribe;*
> *For men and women who nurse;*
> *For surgeons in operating theatres;*
> *For chemists and those who search for healing agencies;*
> *For laboratory workers, who weigh and measure and ponder;*
> *For hospital porters and ambulance men;*

For those who work out diets and prepare them;
For those who give the laying-on-of-hands and anoint the
  sick in Thy Name;
For those who meditate and pray.
Give them diligence, Lord; give them patience; give them
faith. Amen.

✠

Silent Meditation

In quietness and confidence shall be
your strength.

✠

EVENING

MAY I THINK tonight, Lord, not of any troubles of mine,
but rather may my heart be full of praise for Thy
manifest goodness for me, in me, and round me:

I rejoice from my inmost heart at the thought of Thine
eternal infinite Beauty, which is the origin and cause of
all created beauty;
I rejoice at the thought of Thine eternal infinite Love, from
which all other love is come;
I rejoice at Thine eternal Righteousness, by which alone the
light of conscience shines within us;
I rejoice at Thine eternal Truth, which frees us from our
worldly slaveries;
I rejoice at Thine eternal Life, from which we came, by
which we live, and to which we go;
I rejoice at Thine eternal Light, which brings to naught the
powers of darkness;

I rejoice that all this, Thy Goodness, once obscure to men, has for ever been shown forth in the power of Jesus Christ; I rejoice that His Risen Life is ever making new conquests in us over sin, disease and death.

I will rejoice, and sing and give thanks unto Thee, O Lord, with my whole heart. Amen.

☩

To Thy merciful Love, O Lord, I commend this night those whose minds are out of order; those who dwell in the loneliness of mental insufficiency; those who have no earthly friends; those who do not know the comfort of a happy home; those who lie imprisoned; those whose age is a burden to them; the deaf and dumb and blind in hospital, and those who feel they have missed the best in life. May they come to know and trust in Thee, and find their peace in the knowledge of Thy sufficiency. Amen.

☩

Silent Meditation

Be still, and know that I within thee am Life; I will have peace and not turmoil.

THIRTEENTH DAY   *MORNING*

O GOD, Whose merciful ears are always open to my prayers, and Whose nature it is to give me more than I desire, help me to ask only for the things that please Thee. Keep me from seeking the things that hurt, and sustain me in that which is profitable to my soul, for Christ's sake. Amen.

✠

All-ruling and everlasting God, give unto me the increase of faith, hope and charity; and, that I may obtain that which Thou dost promise, make me to love that which Thou dost command; through Jesus Christ our Lord. Amen. (B.C.P.)

✠

O ever-living God, Who by the Resurrection Life of Christ hast given us the hope of that same Life in us, grant me to have the mind which was in Him, that I may show forth in myself the beauty of His wholeness, through the same Jesus Christ our Lord. Amen.

✠

Go forth to thy tasks this day, my soul, in the strength of the Lord God;
Go forth to thy speakings with the Wisdom of His Word;
Go forth to thy doings with the graciousness of His Love;
Go forth to thy plans and thinkings on the ground of His Truth;
Go forth to thy difficulties and decisions with His Peace and His all-Wiseness;

Go forth without doubt or fear; only believe, and thou shalt see that Christ is all in all to thee; only believe, and thou shalt see it come to pass; thy faith shall make thee whole. . . . Lord, I believe. Amen.

✠

Silent Meditation

Whatsoever things you pray and ask for, believe that you have received them, and you shall have them.

EVENING

O FATHER, Who providest all that I could ever need, as I thank Thee for newness of life today, so I pray for its continuance.

As I thank Thee for Thy Presence, I pray that I may know it more deeply.

As I thank Thee for the Light of Thy Spirit restoring me day by day, I pray that I may ever walk in and by that Light.

As I thank Thee for my healing, I pray that I may use my health for Thy glory and for the good of men,

for Christ's sake. Amen.

✠

Help me, Lord, to seek health, and to expect it keenly, not for myself, but for Thee. Purge me from every desire to use my health for purely selfish ends, for my own satisfaction or self-indulgence. Help me to see that as my body is a temple of Thy Spirit, so I must seek for it holiness as well as wholeness. Help me, Lord, to love my body, to treat it well, not for my sake, but for Thine, that Christ may be formed in me more and more, for His sake. Amen.

✠

I thank Thee, Father, for all who have been healed today, whose strength has returned, and who can start their work again, especially —— and —— and ——. Help them to know their debt to Thy Love, and to live for Thee.

And to my sleep, Lord, now I go, for Thou art with me also. Amen.

✠

Silent Meditation

That I may know Him, and the Power
of His Risen Life within me.

FOURTEENTH DAY   *MORNING*

OPEN THOU MINE EYES, O Lord, that I may see the
wondrous things of Thy Law:
Thou hast ordained that Thy people shall be delivered
from every evil;

> *Open my eyes to see it accomplished.*

Thou hast ordained pardon to every penitent;

> *Open my eyes to see it accomplished.*

Thou hast ordained that our diseases should be healed;

> *Open my eyes to see it accomplished.*

Thou hast ordained that Thy Spirit should dwell in us and
give us Life;

> *Open my eyes to see it accomplished.*

Thou hast ordained a Kingdom for us that where Thou art we
may be also;

> *Open my eyes to see it accomplished.*

Thou hast ordained that the earth shall be filled with Thy glory
as the waters cover the sea;

> *Open my eyes to see it accomplished.*

Thou hast ordained that all things shall be possible to him that
believeth;

> *Open my eyes to see it accomplished.*

*Open my eyes, O Lord, to see Thy Laws, Thy Promises,
coming to pass. Open the windows of my soul to see the riches
of Heaven spread before me. Give me the vision to see and
know Thy Goodness perfected in me, and to grasp it with the
hand of faith. Open my heart to let in the warmth of Thy*

healing Love, that it may have its full course in me. For I have remembered Thine everlasting judgements, and have received strength; I will never forget Thy commandments, for with them Thou hast given me life. Amen.

✠

If today, in my weakness, dear Lord, I should feel pain, I know that Thou wilt support me; if I should today fall into fear, Thou wilt still be holding my hand; if today I should be lacking in faith, Thou wilt be there to renew it; if in my frailty today I should forget Thee, Thou wilt never forget me, for Thou hast said, "I will not leave you comfortless. I will come to you." I thank Thee, Jesus. Amen.

✠

Silent Meditation

*I am the Creative Spirit within you,
and in Me there is nothing to fear.*

✠

EVENING

I THANK THEE, Holy Spirit of God, for yet another day of Thy creative energy, never-ceasingly at work in all things. I thank Thee for the evidences of Thy boundless Power, that even I, one humble creature, have seen and known this day, as every day. I thank Thee for Thy Beauty, Thy Wisdom, Thy Holiness, Thy Strength and Peace and Love, unfalteringly in operation in the great universe about me, and yet most marvellously within me also.

Though often, through my sin and folly and pride and self-regard, I have put a barrier between myself and Thy purpose for me; yet through all my wayward blunderings Thy creative Love has ever persisted to work for my good, and works even now.

Eternity is too short to utter all Thy praises, but in this all-too-brief moment of recollection I would give my simple gratitude for increase of grace this day, for growth in health, for newness of being, yea, for the whole work of goodness which Thou hast done, and art doing, in my soul and mind and body. Amen.

☩

Whom have I in Heaven but Thee? And there is none upon earth that I desire, to be compared with Thee. My strength may fail and my heart tremble, but what I have is Thee Thyself, and therefore I dwell in the land of Life. Heaven is about my path and about my bed; awake or asleep I am not separated from Thee. And because Thou livest, Lord Christ, I live also, and shall live. Amen.

☩

Living Jesus, Thou art near,
By Thy Love dispelling fear;
Sleeping not in hours of night,
Thou wilt keep me in Thy Light.
                                        Amen.

☩

Silent Meditation

*I am the Eternal Spirit
creatively at work within
thee.*

FIFTEENTH DAY   *MORNING*

O ETERNAL LORD GOD, Who inhabitest eternity without
ever leaving my side, teach me more and more to
know that if I do not possess Thee, I have nothing,
and that if Thou dost not possess me, I am nothing. Help
me now to open my heart gladly and trustfully to the incoming of the Spirit of Love and Joy and Peace.

Thou hast promised to help me, and I would now accept Thee
at Thy word. When every earthly help fails, that promise still
holds good, and I would ever rely upon it. I do not know
what this day will bring forth, but help me as I go through
its changing hours to turn ever and again to Thee Who
changest not, to draw fresh strength for every need of the day.
Lord, I believe and hope and trust in Thee for all things, for
Thou dost never fail them that seek Thee. Amen.

☩

Inspire me, Loving Father, to seek and to expect health this
day, not for selfish ends, but for unselfish ones.
Let me receive Thy strength, so that I may be strong for the
right;
Let me receive Thy joy, so that I may bring gladness to others;
Let me receive Thy peace, so that I may bring harmony into
Thy world;
Let me receive Thy love, so that I may surrender myself for
others' good;
Let me receive Thy saving health, so that I may be a clear
example of Thy perfect goodness in my every thought and
word and deed, for Christ's sake. Amen.

Silent Meditation

*Stay thy mind on Me, and I will
keep thee in perfect peace.*

☩

EVENING

I DO NOT NEED to ask Thee, Blessed Lord, to abide with me
through the hours of darkness, for Thou hast never left
me, and never wilt. Thou hast graciously promised to
tabernacle with the sons of men. See, Thou art abiding with
me now, as I prepare myself for the night.

The Light which made the sun to shine this day has not
departed with him to leave me comfortless, for when every
sun that is, and each remotest star, shall have vanished into
nothingness, the Light that made them what they are shall still
remain undimmed. So I lay me down in darkness, but my
soul is aglow with Thy Eternal Spirit. All this day Thou hast
been at work in me, and I am the better for it.

Forgive my doubtings of Thy goodness; calm my anxious
thoughts and enable me now to accept in faith Thy promised
peace which passes all understanding. Amen.

☩

In Thy gracious keeping, Father, are all those whose special
needs I think of tonight —— and —— and ——; they are
each intimately known unto Thee, and Thy fatherly hand is
over them for good. May this prayer that I now pray for them
bring to them a greater awareness of Thy love. By our

common faith in Christ I bid their sickness be overcome, in His Name. Amen.

✠

Praise be to Thee, Holy Father, this night, because in my going out and in my coming in Thou art with me, and in my waking and my sleeping, Thou art my comfort. Amen.

✠

Silent Meditation

Through growing faith in Me, Thy Creative Christ, indwelling thee, thou art being made every whit whole.

SIXTEENTH DAY   *MORNING*

Eternal lord god, Thou Eternal Being, without beginning
and having no end, let me now pause, before I enter
upon this new day, and for a moment recollect in Whose
Presence it is that I continually dwell, the Presence that ever
surrounds me with safety and peace.

Let me now, with the darkness of night behind me, put behind
me also all the things which darken my soul. Banish from my
mind every dark thought of hatred, or malice, or ill-will; dis-
perse the shadows of doubt and fear and anxiety; scatter the
clouds of resentment and bitterness and anger. And let Thy
incoming Love spread Light within my heart, so that in me
today men may see an image of Thyself. Amen.

✠

Praise be to Thee, Lord, for Thy beauty, seen in all the
loveliness of Nature;

Praise be to Thee for Thy wisdom, made plain in Thy provi-
dential ordering of all things;

Praise be to Thee for Thy truth, revealed in prophet, sage and
saint, and above all in Jesus Christ;

Praise be to Thee for Thy righteousness, made known in Holy
Scripture;

Praise be to Thee for Thy holiness, most perfectly manifested
in the Incarnation of Thy Son, Christ our Lord. Amen.

✠

Silent Meditation

*That I might be conscious of Thy
healing, uplifting and inspiring
grace in me.*

EVENING

ALL THIS DAY, Loving Father, Thou hast been with me. Thou hast watched over my goings, and held me to the ways of Life, and if I have strayed from Thy Will for me, it has been through my own blindness, or my folly, or my sin, for which I ask now forgiveness.

All this day Thou hast been loving me, and giving me Thy Spirit of life and health; Thou hast been leading me in the way I should go, putting forth Thy strength to renew and restore me.

All this day Thou hast been moving in me to bring to pass that fulness of health which is Thy Will for me.

Possess me now wholly, Lord, and let nothing in me prevent the fulfilment of Thy perfecting work, for Christ's sake. Amen.

☩

I pray tonight for those who are sick in mind;

For those who lack their reason, that they may come to rightness of thinking;

For those in mental homes, that they may be aware of Thy calming Presence;

For those whose damaged minds cause hurt, to themselves or others, that they may come to know Thy peace;

For those who are confused and wandering in their thinking, that they may find the Truth which sets them free;

In Christ's Name I pray that they may all be healed. Amen.

☩

Silent Meditation

I am the Eternal Spirit of
Truth and Peace within you.

SEVENTEENTH DAY   *MORNING*

O LORD JESUS CHRIST, Who didst say, "Whatsoever things ye pray and ask for, believe that ye have received them, and ye shall have them", open now my eyes to see the vision of all things as Thou dost mean them to be.

Help me to see, with the eye of faith, the perfecting of all creation, to see men at one with God and with each other, to see humanity restored in the beauty of wholeness, to see society working according to Thy Divine Plan, to see the New Jerusalem coming down out of Heaven.

Help me to know more deeply that Thou hast willed all these things, and to see that they are even now coming to pass. And give me grace to surrender myself, in all my weakness, to that same Divine Purpose, that I may be alive with Thy likeness, and be satisfied with it, for Thy Name's sake. Amen.

✠

Lord Jesus, Thou Healer of men, I have certain things to ask for myself this day; this —— and this —— and this ——. I know that it is Thy will that I should recover my health, else would I not dare to pray for it.

But I leave this prayer with Thee, for I know that Thou art even now working the answer in me, and that I have already received of Thy goodness. I know that I shall have Thy fulness of health, for I believe that Thou hast given it to me, and that it will be outwardly manifested in me in Thine own good time. I thank Thee, Jesus. Amen.

Bless all those who live with me, and who minister to me out of their love. Give them wisdom, strength and patience, and give me grace gratefully to help them in all they have to do. Amen.

✠

Silent Meditation

That I may become more and more conscious of Thy Creative, Sustaining and Healing Love within me.

✠

EVENING

O ALL-RULING FATHER, Who art the inexhaustible well-spring of all Life, I rejoice that all through the day I have been able to draw upon that Life of Thy Divine Goodness. I praise Thee that as the hours have gone by Thou hast unchangingly imparted to me Thy Peace and Joy, even when I have been too busy with my petty concerns to perceive it. I thank Thee for the gift of health that Thou dost unceasingly pour into me.

Everywhere, Lord, and all the time, Thou hast been busy about Thy gracious work of giving Life, in the trees and flowers, in the birds and beasts, in plant and fruit, in the rolling planets, and even in me.

What am I, Lord, that Thou art thus so thoughtful for me? Praise be to Thee, Loving Lord, that in Christ I have been made to know that I am Thy child, that Thou art verily my

Father; made to know that I shall, therefore, never lack anything that is needful for me. And this day Thou hast given me fresh evidence of Thy care. I have nothing to offer in return that can suffice to match Thy Goodness, nothing but myself, just as I am. Take me, Father, and use me for Thy Kingdom. Amen.

✠

Great Healer of all, I commend to Thee this night all those who are afflicted with sickness that men call incurable; the blind, the lunatic, those with wasting and malignant disease, and all who have resigned themselves to a life of disability. Raise them, Lord, to a vision of Thy Power renewing them. Help them to see all things possible with Thee, and to resign themselves, not to their sickness, but to Thee, that they may find release from the chains of evil to the Freedom of Thy Truth and Peace, for Christ's sake. Amen.

✠

Silent Meditation

I am thy holy and unchanging Life-substance within thee; thou shalt draw thy feeling from Me only.

EIGHTEENTH DAY   MORNING

O FATHER, Whose unflagging energy moves the world and pours light of day upon me, I will wait on Thee now, and renew my strength. I will open my heart to Thine incoming Spirit of Power, so that I may not be weary in my doings this day. Thy grace will uphold me in all I have to do, Thy wisdom will direct me, and I shall be sustained by Thy love. O Unsearchable Goodness, without Thee I can do nothing; with Thee all things are possible unto me. I will rely on Thee now, for Thou never failest to uphold them that rest in Thee. Establish my faith more firmly in Thee, that I may pass this day in confidence and peace, for Christ's sake. Amen.

✠

Thine eye, O Lord, is upon every bird that falls, Thou knowest every hair of my head and Thou hast graven me upon the palms of Thy hands. I am in Thy keeping, and I leave the issues of this day to Thee, knowing that Thou wilt do all things well, in me and for me. Thanks be to Thee, Loving Father. Amen.

✠

There are those, Lord, who enter this day with anxiety, fear, doubt or despair; those whose hearts are full of bitterness and resentment; those to whom this day brings only a renewal of unhappiness. Open their eyes to see Thee and know Thee. Open their hearts to believe that Thou art greater than their hearts, and Master of all their troubles, and help them thus to enter into peace, through Jesus Christ our Lord. Amen.

Silent Meditation

*I am the unfailing source of strength
and peace within you; in Me you
shall have the fulness of life.*

✠

EVENING

O ETERNAL LOVE, I come to the time of sleep, and I turn to Thee in thankfulness for the mercies and blessings of the day. I have lacked for nothing that I needed, for Thou, My God, hast supplied every need, Thou hast filled up every deficiency. I thank Thee for food, clothing, shelter; for home and friends; for life and joy and peace. I thank Thee for growth in health and strength. I thank Thee for all things, for Thy mercies are without number.

And I thank Thee now, Lord, for the precious gift of sleep. Thou wilt be with me during all the hours of darkness, giving new strength to my body. Help me to close my eyes trustfully, knowing that Thou art creatively at work in me, in the night as in the day. If I should wake, let my first thought be of Thy nearness, and in the morning let my chief desire be to serve Thee.

Forgive my sins, Father, by which I have this day shut out Thy Light. Forgive my wilful disobedience to Thy known commandments. Forgive this —— and this —— and this ——, and accept my humble thanks for the pardon Thou hast freely offered me in Christ Jesus. Amen.

Freely now, Lord, I forgive any who have hurt, offended or wronged me. Help me in forgiving, also to forget; help me to love them who love me not, and in loving them to show my love for Thee. Save me from imagined wrongs, and make me look always for the good in all men, for Christ's sake. Amen.

✠

Silent Meditation

That I may enter more and more fully into awareness of Thy creative and healing love within me.

NINETEENTH DAY   *MORNING*

BLESSED LORD JESUS, praise be to Thee for Thy compassionate Love which healed the souls and bodies of men, women and children in the days of Thy flesh. Glory and praise to Thee for making the deaf to hear and the dumb to speak; for giving sight to the blind and making palsied limbs to move; for restoring the penitent and retrieving the lost; for giving new purpose to aimless lives; for comforting the sorrowing and raising the dead.

Praise to Thee, dear Lord, for this wondrous Gospel of God's healing Love which Thou hast made plain to us. But above all praise to Thee that Thou hast never ceased this redeeming work, but hast ever continued down the ages to lay Thine hand for healing upon faithful souls, and because Thou art even now present with us to heal, to work all Thy miracles of grace in them that believe.

Lord, I believe Thy word, that Thou art with me, to make me whole. Come then, Lord, and heal me every whit, in body, mind and soul, so that I may praise Thee, not only with my lips, but with my whole being, now and always. Amen.

✠

Bless all those, Lord Jesus, whose work it is to preach the Gospel, Thy Good News. Help them to make real to Thy people the power of the saving, wholesome message, that it may be received with joy. Bless all who hear the Word, that they may open their hearts to the knowledge of Thy healing Love, and walk faithfully in it, for Thy glory and their own salvation. Amen.

Silent Meditation

*I will renew thy consciousness with
the knowledge of My incoming Spirit
of Life and Love.*

✠

EVENING

I THANK THEE, Father, for the hours that are gone, and for all the goodness they have brought me. I thank Thee for the grace which has enabled me to do such good as I have tried to do. Forgive me for the opportunities for good that I have missed, through sin, neglect or carelessness. I thank Thee for the help of neighbours, the kindliness of friends, and the love of my relations. I thank Thee for the life and health Thou hast given me, and which Thou art maintaining in me now. And as I pray thankfully, help me also to live thankfully, with love and joy and peace in my every word and deed, at all times, for all men. Amen.

✠

Lord, my trust is in Thee, my soul hangs upon Thee, and all my hope is in Thy promises. No evil shall happen unto me that can overcome me, for Thou art my Shield. Amen.

✠

Lord Jesus, I pray that Thy Church everywhere may be faithful to the ministry of healing with which Thou hast entrusted it. May its ministers go forth with confidence in Thy Name to bring healing grace to all who need it. May its congregations be alive with trust in Thy healing power, that they may be storehouses of Thy renewing life. May those who are sick seek Thy healing hand, and may people more and more desire health of soul as well as of body, that they may seek to glorify Thee with Thy precious gift of wholesome life, so that Thy Kingdom may come on earth as it is in Heaven, where with the Father of all goodness and the Holy Spirit of Life Thou livest and reignest in love for ever. Amen.

☩

Silent Meditation

*I acknowledge Thee, and Thee only,
as my Health-producing Power and
Wisdom. Thee only will I serve.*

TWENTIETH DAY   *MORNING*

H ERE, Great Lord of Lords, is another day; here am I; and here art Thou, filling the world with daylight, and me with Thine Eternal Light. I acknowledge Thee to be my Life, creatively present within me. I open the doors of my heart once more, willingly and gladly, to Thine incoming Spirit of Wisdom and Power. Once more I acknowledge Thee to be my only source of Health, for Thou art my beginning and my end. Thou art my portion, O Lord, and Thou hast dealt graciously with me, and this day Thy goodness will still be with me, Thy Love will not pass me by. Thanks be to Thee, Lord, for this new day. Amen.

✠

F ather, I pray to Thee for health, because Thou art Health. I pray for health of soul and body, because I would be whole; I would be perfect, as Thou, my Father in Heaven, art perfect. I pray for health confidently, because Thou hast taught me to bring all my needs to Thee. I pray for health without anxiety, for I know that Thou art always present to heal. And I pray for health without impatience, for I know that Thou wilt open the doors to fulness of life in Thine own good time, and lead me where Thou wouldst have me be. Whatever else the day may bring, I believe that it will also bring Thy joy, and with that I am content. Amen.

✠

S ave me, Lord, this day, from anger and irritability, save me from malice and meanness, and from any unloving word or deed, for Christ's sake. Amen.

Silent Meditation

*Infinite Spirit of Wisdom within,
come forth and direct me in all the
ways of my self-conscious life.*

✠

EVENING

O ALL-PROVIDENT GOD, Thou art the God, not of the dead, but of the living; the God of Abraham, Isaac and Jacob, Who hast guided man from his primeval beginnings, out of his savage darkness, to place his feet on the road that leads to life, and Who hast led him surely along his upward road, and illumined him with the Light of Christ.

Thou art He who created us for perfection. Thou art He Who in Christ hast opened the way to it for all men. Thou art He Whose Spirit daily fills us with Thine Own creative life. Take the praise of this my soul, which acknowledges Thine unsearchable greatness, yet rejoices in Thy ceaseless nearness. Praise and glory be to Thee, Thou indestructible life within me. Thou art the God of Life, even of my life also, and in Thee is all my health, my joy and my sure salvation. Amen.

✠

O Christ, Prince of Peace and lover of souls, I pray for all those in whose hands is the peace of the nations. May they seek, not their own good, but each the good of others. May they allow Thy Eternal Spirit of Wisdom and Truth to break forth in all their counsels. May they learn to quell suspicions and fears.

Draw together nations which distrust each other, and help them to resolve their difficulties in the spirit of charity, and may the peoples of the world be led forth into the blessed peace of the children of God. Thou art the God Whose Spirit ordereth all things sweetly, and in Thee only are we at peace. Heal the nations, Lord; bind up their wounds; give them light in their blindness, and raise them in peace upon their feet to walk together in brotherhood, in the freedom of Thy service. Amen.

✠

Silent Meditation

I am Thy Holy Spirit of knowledge,
thy High Counsellor within.

TWENTY-FIRST DAY   *MORNING*

O LORD of all loveliness, help me this and every day to delight in the beauty of Thy creation:

Thou hast made the sun to step down his golden pathways, and the moon by night to spread her silver curtain;

Thy faultless fingers have fashioned the velvet firmament and dusted it with stars;

Each blade of grass and every rustling tree is what it is because of Thee;

Each rain-drop hides a rainbow, and the snow-flake shimmers in a symmetry beyond conceit of men;

The blue of sky, the green of earth and the flame of evening sun are all Thy thoughts;

There is no rose, nor soaring lark-song, nor tossing field of corn, but tells its tale of Thine enchanting Mind;

Wherever I look, Thy treasure-house of beauty lays wide its doors before me, and in us, Thy human fashioning, lie beauties of the mind and soul, placed there by Thee, wherewith we may see and love Thine inexhaustible loveliness.

Thy Beauteous Spirit stirs within me, Lord. Let Him come forth in me now, to overcome all ugliness in me of word or work or will. Help me myself to be an image of Thy Beauty, that some glimpses of Thy glory may be known in me today. Amen.

Lord Jesus, Who didst bid us be like children, that we might enter into Thy Kingdom, I commend to Thee all little children, especially those who are dear to me. Grant that all who will influence them today may guard their minds from all dark thoughts and evil ideas. Lead them in the ways of Thy light and joy and gladness, for Thy dear Name's sake. Amen.

✠

Silent Meditation

*I am the Life, and the Life is the
Light of men.*

✠

EVENING

O EVER-WISE GOD, Thou art the all-Knowing Power within me; Thou knowest all my needs, and how best to fulfil them. Thus, day by day, Thou art renewing my body, re-building fresh cells and tissue, and so daily strengthening me. I trust myself to Thee for the healing of my body.

But, Lord, Thou knowest also my deeper spiritual needs, needs of which I may be ignorant, or which I try to hide. Help me by Thine indwelling Spirit to know my inner weaknesses, to understand my spiritual defects, to become aware of the faults and failings which hinder Thy healing grace. Enlighten me so that I may not be blind to any evil in me; show me my wrong attitudes, my unspoken prejudices, my deep unconscious selfishness.

Help me to know myself with Thy knowing. Let Thy Love show me myself as I am, and heal the evil in me. Regenerate me, Father, the real inner me. Let me become joyfully aware of the Divine Love, which burns and purges. Let me be crucified with Christ, and join Him on the Cross of self-emptying, that there may be no room within me but for the cleansing fire of Thy Love.

Give me the new birth, Lord, which is after the fashioning of Thy Holy Spirit. So, Lord, as I trust myself to Thee for the healing of this body, so do I trust Thee for the healing of my soul, which Thou hast made to dwell with Thee for ever and ever. Amen.

☥

I thank Thee, Father, for the night, whereby Thou hast taught us to trust Thee even when we are in darkness, or are helpless, or are walking in the valley of the shadow of death, for in all these Thou art still our Life. Amen.

☥

Silent Meditation

I will be unto thee an everlasting light.

TWENTY-SECOND DAY   *MORNING*

L ORD JESUS, I would renew my faith in Thee.

    Thou hast said:

He that heareth My word, and believeth Him that sent Me,
hath eternal life, and hath passed out of death into life.

                           Lord, I believe.

Thou hast said:

They that hear the voice of the Son of God shall live.

                           Lord, I believe.

Thou hast said:

The Son of Man shall give unto you the meat which abideth
unto eternal life.

                           Lord, I believe.

Thou hast said:

He that followeth me shall have the light of life.

                           Lord, I believe.

Thou hast said:

I came that they may have life in abundance.

                           Lord, I believe.

Thou hast said:

I know My sheep, and I give unto them eternal life, and
they shall never perish.

                           Lord, I believe.

Thou hast said:

I am the Resurrection and the Life: he that believeth on
me, though he die, yet shall he live.

                           Lord, I believe.

Lord Jesus, in the face of all that this fallen world can bring,
sin, sorrow, sickness and death, I still firmly stand upon the

feet of faith, faith that in Thee is the very essence of Life, and that Thy Life in me is conquering every evil. I cannot leave Thee, Lord. To whom would I go? Thou hast the words of Eternal Life; freely dost Thou offer it to me, and freely I accept it. Amen.

☩

Silent Meditation

I am Eternal Goodness within thee.

☩

EVENING

THANKS BE TO THEE, Holy Father, for the revelation of Thyself as the Healing God given to us in Jesus Christ, Who went about doing good;

Thanks for the calming touch of His hand on the anxious, the deaf and dumb, the fevered brow, the broken nerve and the weakened brain;

Thanks for the calming touch of His hand on the anxious the sorrowful and the fearful;

Thanks for the glorious and joyful Truth in Him, which at a word set free our spirits for ever from all the bondage of sin and sickness, from the slavery of all false thinking and teaching;

Thanks be to Thee, Holy Father, for that Thou hast enabled even me to enter, by faith in Him, the way of Truth and Life, the way to Thee, my strength and my sufficiency. Amen.

Lord Jesus, Thou hast put Thy Spirit in me, and I am no more in bondage to the flesh, and Thy Spirit, which could not be held by death, but brought Thee from the grave to make for us an everlasting Easter, shall also quicken my mortal body, so that I may for ever live, not after the flesh, but after the Spirit. Enable me now and always to suffer all things with Thee, that I may be also glorified with Thee, to Whom be all glory in the Church, in the world, and in me. Amen.

☩

In the stillness of the evening, O Father-God, I would still my mind and heart, to become aware of Thy all-pervading Presence; I would cast out of me all the warring emotions, all the fiery darts of evil within, all the disharmony, all the poisons which disturb the mind. And I would become increasingly conscious of the reality of Thy Peace round me and in me. I would close my eyes to all outward things, and know the only Truth, Thyself, dwelling within me, giving me harmony, unity, and the strength of Thy peace. Amen.

☩

Silent Meditation

Trust Thou in Me, thy Infinite Health within.

E

TWENTY-THIRD DAY   *MORNING*

A GAIN THE DAY COMES, my Father, with its promise of Thy mercies. Whatsoever I shall need today, I shall need Thee more, for there is nothing that I can long for that is not to be found in Thee. Therefore, Lord, deepen my desire for Thee alone. Help me, as this day runs its course, to fix the eye of my mind on Thee, to turn my ear to the gracious words Thou hast spoken to me: *Thou art Mine.*

Even in the midst of sickness and pain, should they befall me, yet will not my heart be afraid, for what Thou hast been to men of old, so art Thou to me now. Thou truly art my strength and my salvation; Thou art my defence so that I shall not fall; Thou art my health and my glory, the unshakeable rock on which my strength stands. In Thee is my trust, and so shall it be all this day. Amen.

✠

Enable me, Lord, to follow the way of healing love today:

That I may be long-suffering and kind;
That I may not be envious, nor vaunt myself;
That I may not be puffed up, nor behave myself unseemly;
That I may not seek my own selfish ends, nor allow myself to be provoked;
That I may not look for, nor allow any importance to, any evil;
That I may take no pleasure in anything that is not right, but rejoice only in what is true;
That I may bear all things, believe all things, hope all things;
That even when faith falls low, and hope is dim, I may yet abide in love.

Then I shall lack nothing, for I shall abide in Thee, and Thou art Love itself. Amen.

☩

Silent Meditation

Because I live, ye shall live also:
there is nothing impossible to the
Life within you.

☩

EVENING

LORD JESUS, Who hast taught us that the work of God is to believe on Thee Whom He hath sent, I would renew my belief in the Divine Goodness. Give me Thy grace day by day to believe upon my Heavenly Father, to reverence Him, and to love Him, with all my heart, and mind, and soul and strength; to worship Him, to give Him thanks, to put my whole trust in Him, to call on Him believingly, to honour above all else His Holy Name and Word, and to serve Him truly all my days. Amen.

☩

Lord Jesus, I accept Thee as my Saviour, my Healer. I accept Thee as the Light which lightens me, as my daily sustenance, as my High Counsellor, as my ever-present Companion and Friend. I rely on Thee for the Life that upholds, inspires and quickens, and Thou wilt not disappoint me. Many times I have disappointed Thee this day, by this —— and this —— and this ——. Yet in spite of all my undeservings, Thy love will not let me go. As I acknowledge with shame my own misdeeds, so help me to receive with gratitude Thy pardon and peace and renewal. Amen.

Bless, O Lord, and lead to their salvation, those whose eyes are blind to Thy Glory, those whose ears are deaf to Thy Word, those whose hearts are cold to Thy Love, those whose souls are paralysed from serving Thee, and those whose minds are captivated by any evil; bless them, Lord, and bring them to Truth, for Thy dear Name's sake. Amen.

✠

Silent Meditation

I am the Resurrection and the Life within thee.

TWENTY-FOURTH DAY *MORNING*

Loving father, Thou hast brought me in safety to the beginning of this day, because Thou hast still a purpose for me to fulfil, a work for me to do, a witness for me to make. Help me, therefore, to put aside any worries or fears, and to open my heart to Thy promptings, to surrender my will to be guided by Thine.

Thou hast wondrously led me to faith in Thee by Jesus Christ, and art filling me even now with all joy and peace in believing, making me to abound in hope, by the power of Thy Holy Spirit dwelling within me.

May Thy grace find full course in me this day, that I may show forth true joyfulness, even in the most ordinary circumstances of my daily occupation, yea, most especially in those circumstances; bind all the happenings of this day with the golden cord of Thy Peace, through Christ the Prince of Peace. Amen.

☧

Lord Jesus, Who hast opened the gates of my prison of anxiety and doubt, and enabled me to walk in the light with shining certainty of my Father's goodness, I put myself in Thy hands this morning, and will abide in Thy keeping for the rest of the day, knowing that thereby I shall be able to live its hours in strength and gladness. Amen.

☧

Use me today, Lord, to bring peace. Make me to be so conscious of Thy Peace within me, that as I speak to others, that peace may be in my words. When I go into the company of men and women, may my coming bring with it an atmosphere of peace. May my presence in any place spread harmony and concord. Use me as a bridge of peace between those who are out of tune with each other, or with Thee. Make me one of Thy peacemakers, Lord, that I may be truly the child of God. Amen.

✠

Silent Meditation

*Teach me Thy way of living, O
Christ my Master within me.*

✠

EVENING

I WOULD BE STILL, Holy God, and be aware of Thy Presence, the Power that lies behind the whole universe, the Power that for ever is, and ceases not, yet dwells with me now. I would be still, Spirit of Life, Who movest all things in rhythmic order and perfect sequence, and Who movest also in me to bring about in me the wholeness which is in Thyself. I would be still, Holy God, and be aware of Thy Presence.

Thank you, Holy Father. Amen.

✠

And now, Lord, lest I invite Thee into an unworthy room, cleanse my heart and mind of the things which hinder Thy coming in. Wash away my cherished resentments, the bitter, backward-looking thoughts of hurts long past. Sweep clean, with the rushing wind of Thy Eternal Spirit, the dusty corners of my mind, still dark with memories of frustration and defeat. Dispel the gloom of any fear or anger, of any doubt or difficulty, which may surround me now. Save me from any animosity towards my fellow-creatures. And save me, Lord, from any hard thoughts of Thee. Cleanse the room of my soul; absolve me now, for Jesus' sake. Amen.

☩

O Holy Spirit, fill me with the truth of God's boundless Love for every soul of His making, and for me;
Upon this truth would I lean with all my heart.

Fill me with the truth that my Heavenly Father is upholding me with the wisdom that ordains the stars in their courses;
Upon this truth would I lean with all my heart.

Fill me with the truth that His everlasting compassion is fixed on me, even in my very sinfulness;
Upon this truth would I lean with all my heart.

Fill me with the truth that His providence is guiding all my steps, holding my hand, and daily renewing me with His own perfect Life;
Upon this truth would I lean with all my heart. Amen.

☩

Silent Meditation

*You shall know the Truth, and the
Truth shall make you free.*

TWENTY-FIFTH DAY   *MORNING*

L ORD JESUS, Who didst teach us how to be truly blessed, help me to seek happiness after Thy fashion:

Let me be humble-minded, that I may know the blessedness of possessing the Kingdom of Heaven;

Let me ardently long for the coming of Thy Kingdom, that I may know the blessedness of being given courage and comfort in my longing;

Let me claim nothing, that I may know the blessedness of having all things;

Let me hunger and thirst for goodness, that I may know the blessedness of being fully satisfied;

Let me be kind in heart, that I may know the blessedness of a heart at peace;

Let me be pure in heart, that I may know the blessedness of enjoying the vision of God;

Let me be a peace-maker, that I may know the blessedness of God's own child;

Let me seek righteousness, even if I suffer for it, that I may know the blessedness of belonging to the Kingdom. Amen.

✠

H elp me, Lord Jesus, so to be emptied of self, that I may be filled with Thee. Let me be blessed with the blessedness of that great company of saints who found true life by losing it in Thee. Let me be happy with the happiness found, not in the things of this world, but in singleness of heart. Let my restless heart find rest in Thee, that I may know the blessedness of inner peace.

When life about me seems stale and uninteresting, may I be as the salt of the earth. When the world about me walks in darkness, let me be as a light, to bring hope and joy and peace and strength to all with whom I have to do. Through all the hours of this day. Lord Jesus, may I both know, and be a channel of, Thy Blessing. Amen.

✠

Silent Meditation

*Thou shalt be quickened and illumined
by the incoming of My Love.*

✠

EVENING

HOLY FATHER, unsleeping Lord of all things, again I come to the quiet of evening; the hurry of the day is over, night has laid her curtain of stillness upon the bustling activity of the busy hours. Thou hast brought me safely to the time of rest. Place Thy quieting Hand upon me. Let my heart and mind also be still. I am aware now of Thy silent, calming Presence, and enter into the stillness of Thy Divine activity. I turn again to Thee to experience the sureness of Thy support. I rest once more on Thy strength, Thou Who art unmoved, yet ever moving in me.

✠

Quiet, then, all my troubled thoughts. Set my anxious fretfulness against the overcoming Power of Thy Divine Love, and let me see how little are my worries, how puny are my fears. Wherever I am, Father, there art Thou, for see! from day to day, yea, from everlasting to everlasting Thou hast loved me, and wilt love me, and wilt not be swerved from Thy purpose to save and to heal me. I thank Thee, Father. Amen.

Holy Being, the Uncreated One, Who wast, and art, and shalt ever be, Thou didst make all things, and me, because Thou art very Life, the substance of all that is. Thy Divine energy is ceaselessly pouring love upon me, day by day making me into Thy Divine likeness, day by day overcoming in me the enemies of Thy Goodness. Let it burn away with its cleansing fire every destructive thought and feeling. Purge out of me any spirit of condemnation and blaming of others. Save me from being contemptuous, from despising others, from mean or malicious judgments.

Empty me of any desire to minister to my self-esteem, or to outshine other people. Help me to show by my life that humility cometh before honour. So cleanse me, Lord, of all that exalts myself, that my soul may be a ready room for the habitation of Thy Holy Love. So purge me of self-regard that Thy Love may pour through me to be shed abundantly on others. For Thy sake, Father, I would love my neighbour more. Amen.

✠

Silent Meditation

I would be conscious of Thy Creative
Spirit in heart and mind.

TWENTY-SIXTH DAY   *MORNING*

LORD JESUS, Who wast Master of all things because Thou wast one with the Father, I would enter more and more into that same one-ness. Here at the beginning of another day, before I engage in its activities, I would be freed of everything which separates me from my Father. Here I cast aside all doubts and denials of His Goodness, all feelings of despondency and despair. Here I would cast aside all the hurts and wounds of heart and mind, all the outward things which try to destroy my trust in Him. Here, too, I cast aside all my negative thinking and emotion, all my impatience and irritability, all my resentment and temper, and every feeling of jealousy and rebellion which my heart may have harboured from former days.

And, as I cast aside, also, any fears which darken the outlook of this day, teach me, Master of all, to fear nothing at all but separation from the Good Father. Deepen in me the knowledge that my highest good for body and soul is to be in harmony with Him. O Thou, my Saviour, Who wast born into the world of time, that Thou mightest bring to us sons of men the eternal light of the Good God, be Thou born in me, that I may have the mastery over all un-God-like motives, desires, words and acts.

Capture me wholly, that Thy one-ness with the Father may be my portion also. Make me so at-one with Him that all disease, discord and disharmony may be done away. Let this day be one of unbroken union with the source of all Life and Light. Be born again, Lord Jesus, be born again, in me. Amen.

Lord Jesus, help me this day to be a clear channel of Thy forgivingness. Help me to bring the spirit of forgiveness to all men. Especially help me to be charitable and forgiving to those I do not like. To all who are difficult, or awkward, or offensive, make me to extend a loving heart. Kindle in me the flame of compassion towards those who go wrong, those who are different from me, those who irritate or hinder me. Help me so to love all men that I may have no enemies in my heart. Give me the great heart, that I may cast about all men the all-including mantle of understanding charity. Let me bring to this day Thine Own healing forgiveness. Amen.

✠

Silent Meditation

*That I may grow daily in the knowledge of
Thy Power within me.*

✠

EVENING

I PLACE before Thee, Compassionate Father, all that this day has been: and first I would thank Thee:

*For all that has been good in it, the goodness in the world around me, and for all the signs of Thy Life;
For the goodness in other people which I have known in their life today, in their words and in their deeds;
For the goodness in Thyself, the goodness that Thou art, and which has been working in me;
For any goodness which I have been able to show, I thank*

Thee, too, because without Thee I could not have shown it.
Deepen in me the awareness of Thy goodness, and increase
in me the spirit of gratitude. Amen.

And, Good Lord, I place before Thee all the things whereby I have this day been made to feel inadequate, weak or frustrated; all the experiences which have annoyed me; which have hurt or offended me, or which have cast a shadow over the passing hours; anything which has set me at cross purposes. All these, Father, I give Thee now, for in Thy sight they are but little, and against Thy Mighty Love they count for naught. Praise be to Thee, all-sufficient Father. Amen.

I commend to Thy Love, dear Lord, those who tonight are bearing burdens of the spirit, whose daily life is full of trouble, who live in unhappy homes, or to whom life brings hardship, hurtfulness and misery. I give into Thy keeping any who are persecuted, or made to suffer by unkindliness, all who are in need of tenderness and gentle hands, and find them not. May this prayer bring them, on the unseen pathways of the spirit, some knowledge of Thy nearness, some awareness of Thy Healing Peace. Amen.

✠

Silent Meditation

Be still, and know the quickening Power of
My Joy within thee.

TWENTY-SEVENTH DAY　　　　　　　　*MORNING*

BLESSED LORD JESUS, I give thanks once again for my safe-coming to the morning light. I rejoice in Thy nearness to me at the start of another day, for in Thy Presence is the fulness of joy. Enable me today to fight manfully in the battle against all evil. Keep before me the knowledge that my wrestling is not against flesh and blood, but against spiritual evil, against the powers of darkness within and without. I am not able to fight that battle, Lord Jesus, in my own strength, but I can do it in Thine, for from Thee are given all the weapons of the heavenly warfare. Gird upon me, there-fore, ever more firmly, the armour of God.

Surround me with the girdle of Truth, to make me this day true in all my dealings, true in thought and word and deed, true to Thee, true to my fellow-men;

Put on me Thy Righteousness as a breastplate to go forward in the name of Goodness, never turning my back upon the enemies of right, not trying to escape the issues, but facing them out whatever may result. Let me not temporise with evil, or compromise between right and wrong today;

Make me to walk confidently, shod with the Gospel of Peace, so that I may fear no hurt in my goings, and that my journey-ings may be those of an evangelist, taking everywhere with me the Good News of Thy prevailing Love;

Give me a firmer grip on faith, that it may be a shield that cannot be torn away, that all evil that may approach me may be powerless to hurt;

Let the Word of God be to me as sword is to hand, a ready weapon to destroy all falsehood, all evil purposes and plans, all wrong thoughts and attitudes;

And set upon me the protection of Thy Salvation, as a helmet, that I may know of a surety that I am guarded by Thy wholeness.

Thus fortified by Thy Power, in me and around me, Lord, I face the day gladly. Protected by Thine armour of Heaven, and with Thy Word in my heart, I cannot be cast down. Amen.

⊹

Silent Meditation

Thou shalt be more and more aware of My
Creative, regenerating Spirit within thee.

⊹

EVENING

O MIGHTY FATHER, The Eternal One, in Whom is all goodness, and in Whom all goodness is eternal, in Whom all perfection ever was, is, and shall be, I open my heart now to the knowledge that Truth is Eternal, and that all evil is but the creation of sin, and is to be destroyed.

Help me to see beyond the disorder which men make, and to behold Thy Divine Order;
     To this I lift my faith again, Father.

Help me to see beyond the hate which men arouse, and to behold the Divine, uncreated Love;
     To this I lift my faith again, Father.

Help me to see beyond the fear which men in their blindness stir up, and to behold Thy Divine Providence;
     To this I lift my faith again, Father.

Help me to see beyond the unhappiness which men create by

wilful self-concern, and to behold Thy Divine out-going goodness;

> *To this I lift my faith again, Father.*

Help me to see beyond the discord made by men's unruly
hearts, and to behold Thy Divine, unchanging Peace;

> *To this I lift my faith again, Father.*

Help me to see beyond the diseases of men's souls and minds
and bodies, brought on by the world's sin, and to behold Thy
Divine wholeness and health which ever is;

> *To this I lift my faith again, Father.*

O Holy, Uncreated Loveliness, teach me to know more surely
that evil is but transient, that because it is not made by Thee,
but by the folly and waywardness of men, it will be overcome
by the very fact of Thine everlastingness. Help me to break
free from slavery to this world's evil things. I open my eyes to
the sights and sounds of the unseen world around, that I may
bring back to this world something of its strength and beauty.
May the glory of Heaven shine about my path and about my
bed, always. Amen.

✠

Silent Meditation

> *I am All-knowing Love, thy Origin and End.*
> *Be still, and know the blessedness of unity*
> *with Me.*

TWENTY-EIGHTH DAY   *MORNING*

I WAKEN AGAIN to a life full of Thee, Thou great Lord. Round me pulses ceaselessly the unseen rhythm of Thy creative Power, in all things, through all things. In me, too, Thy gentle might moves on, silently surging through all the hours to re-create me in Thy perfect image.

Lord, I pause to refresh myself in this great thing, that the Uncreated Spirit, by Whom all things began, and by Whom they go on to their appointed destiny, dwells even in me, one humble child of God. Thou hast made me to share in Him who broods o'er all things, and in me is some portion of Thy mighty Life. And here, at the doorway of another day I stand, to open my heart and mind anew to the inflowing Life which is from Thee, that in me today Thou mightest order all things well, and fashion my doings according to Thine Own sure Wisdom.

Lord, I plight my troth to Thee again; again I renew my allegiance to Thee; again I return myself to Thy service, for I am Thine. Bless me with a continued sense of Thy Living Presence as I go about the day's business. Help me, as I go through the hours of time, to dwell in spirit beyond the bounds of time. Help me, in the midst of change and chance, to remember that I dwell in the realm of unchanging Life and Love. Let no anxiety or fret chain me, no pain or weakness hold me fast, nor any temptation bring me to my knees except in prayer. May I be fully alive this day with Thy Life, that Thy Kingdom may come in me today, and Thy will be done. Amen.

Lord, I will fear naught today, for I am still the object of Thy
    Love.
  I will fear no alarm, for Thy Presence will still it;
  I will fear no loss, for Thou wilt replace it;
  I will fear no pain, for Thou wilt o'ercome it;
  I will fear no disappointment, for Thou wilt provide some
    better thing;
  I will fear no enemy, for Thou dost love him, too;
  I will fear no difficulty, for Thy strength will meet it;
  I will fear no problem, for Thy wisdom will show the way.

Holy Father, Thou knowest all things, and that which is to
come is not hid from Thee. I place the day to come in Thy
keeping. In the stillness of the morning I resign all the hours
ahead to Thee, and know that all things shall be well with me,
for nothing can separate me from Thy Love. Amen.

⊹

Silent Meditation

Be still, and thou shalt know me as thy
Health-producing Power and Wisdom.

⊹

EVENING

Lord jesus, Who for our sakes became poor, that through
    Thy poverty we might become rich, teach me to live as
    having nothing, that I might possess all things. Show
me how to lose life in such wise as to find it, how to bear
sorrow with joy in my heart, how to be poor while making
many rich, how to be pressed on every side without being
straitened, how to be perplexed without despairing.

While I live among the things of the world, which pass away, let me not depend on them for my happiness, but let my treasure be in Heaven. Renew my inward man day by day, and set my eyes on things not seen, that gleam with eternal glory. For my true life is hid, O Christ, in Thee, and no matter what this world may deny me, I have in Thee that which passeth not away. In Thee I am rich beyond measure. I thank Thee, Jesus. Amen.

I thank Thee, Father, for the light within which guides my steps, Thy voice which checks, reproves, and guards the way of Life, for the Spirit which leads me in the truth. Guided by that light, prompted by that voice, led by that truth, I would acknowledge now my failings today. Let me not try to hide them, nor to excuse my fallings-back, but give me the courage and humility to admit my sins, this —— and this —— and this ——.

Teach me to know that my sins separate me from Thee, and bar the entrance of Thy Spirit of Life into my soul. Help me to see that my waywardness hinders the work of Thy healing grace. But help me also, Lord, not to hold on to the memory of my faults, nor to be tormented by them.

Here I acknowledge gladly Thy full forgiveness, and put the past behind me. In this newness of life I can start afresh at peace. In the victory of our Lord Christ Thou hast defeated all evil and the power thereof. I thank Thee, Father, for Thine absolving Love. **Amen.**

☩

Silent Meditation

Let Thy Truth and Thy Loving-kindness
continually preserve me.

TWENTY-NINTH DAY   *MORNING*

O PERFECT FATHER, with deep desire I desire to be healed, to be healed of every ignorant emotion, of every ignorant thought, of every ignorant sensation. With deep desire I desire to be made whole, healed of all the thoughts which hinder Thy Truth from taking possession of my mind, healed of every false feeling which hinders Thy Love from taking possession of my heart, healed of every physical sensation which hinders Thy Power from taking possession of my body.

So I come to Thee, for Thou art the Source of all health and healing. I thank Thee that Thou art even now answering my desire, as deep calls to deep, for I know that it is not I who have to wait for Thee to give, but Thou Who waitest for me to receive. Here I am, Father; I would receive Thy gifts. Amen.

✠

Father, I look to Thee for health of body, and I know that Thou wouldest heal me. Let my body be Thy servant.

I look to Thee for health of mind, and I know that Thou understandest me. Let my mind think Thy thoughts.

I look to Thee for health of soul, and I know that Thy will is to redeem it for ever. Let my soul be set to do Thy will.

I look to Thee for wholeness every whit, Lord, and I thank Thee that Thou hast heard me. Amen.

✠

I pray, too, Father, for all men's healing as for my own, knowing that Thy will is to heal. Save us from impatience of delay, from despair in apparent disappointment, from irritation when the way seems long, from woeful questionings when the voice of Heaven seems silent. Give us the long sight of faith, to know that Thy Love has no bounds of time or space, and that Thine all-sufficient answer to our need is already lying in the hand of Thy timeless Providence.

I thank Thee, Father, for the healing that is, and is to be.

Amen.

☩

Silent Meditation

Call upon Me, thy Creative Spirit within, and I will answer thee. Thou art in My keeping, and in Me there is nothing to fear.

☩

EVENING

HOLY SPIRIT, Lord of Life, Master of the powers of darkness, Thou art He that sees and knows and understands all things;
I put my trust in Thee.

Holy Spirit, by Whom cometh the breath of all things living, Thou art He that dwells within me also;
I put my trust in Thee.

Holy Spirit, Who bringest all things to perfection, Thou art He that brings order out of chaos, and heals the hurts of men;
I put my trust in Thee.

Holy Spirit, Who sheddest abroad the Love of God in our hearts, Thou art He that shields us in the storms of life;
I put my trust in Thee.

Holy Spirit, Who proceedest from the Eternal Strength of God, Thou art He that gives power to weak men to do God's will;

I put my trust in Thee.

Holy Spirit, Who fillest the bounds of Eternity, Thou art He that enfolds us mortals with Divine protection;

I put my trust in Thee.

Holy Spirit, Lord of my life and guide of my soul, I relinquish all my fears and worries, all my troubles and anxieties, and trust myself to Thy keeping for all the hours of night, and all the days to come. Amen.

☩

Silent Meditation

By the Inspiration of My Spirit I heal thee now of every feeling that is contrary to my Love.

THIRTIETH DAY   MORNING

As day succeeds to day, Holy Father, so let prayer succeed to prayer. Help me always to pray and never to lose heart. Help me to be persistent and steadfast in my comings to the Throne of Grace. Teach me to know that Thou dost never refuse an answer to my prayer, but that the chiefest hindrance lies in me. Help me to continue patiently in prayer until the hindrance is done away, so that Thy will for me may be brought to pass. Amen.

I surrender to Thee discouragement and disappointment,
  And Thou fillest me with Thy sufficiency;
I surrender to Thee wrong habits of thought, and untamed desires,
  And Thou givest me Thy Freedom;
I surrender to Thee my pride and self-regard,
  And Thou givest me Thy meek spirit;
I surrender to Thee my fear and impatience,
  And Thou givest me Thy Peace;
I surrender to Thee my urgent self-seeking,
  And Thou fillest me with knowledge of Thy Will;
I give up to Thee my unforgiving spirit and hardness of heart,
  And Thou givest me Thy Love;
My insincere professions and my half-desires of service I surrender,
  And Thou givest me Thy Truth;
All my selfish graspings after what pleases only me, I hand over, Lord, and my unwillingness to see the needs of others,
  And Thou givest me of Thine Own Goodness;
I surrender to Thee my ignorance and prejudice, and my un-readiness to understand,
  And Thou givest me Light. Amen.

Lord Jesus, Incarnate Love of God, Thou art the Tree of Life, whose leaves are for the healing of men, ceaselessly bearing fruit in them to newness of soul and mind and body. I am in the path of Thy Love, and I rejoice to know Thy Life at work within me. I will tread the road of this day unafraid, and confident of Thy Power within. Bring me to the peace of evening some way nearer to my perfecting. Amen.

✠

Silent Meditation
Lift up thy heart, for I am with thee to strengthen, cleanse and quicken thee.

✠

EVENING

Inspire me, Giver of all Goodness, with a spirit of gratitude for this day's mercies. Let me be deeply aware now of what Thou hast done, and art doing, for me and in me. Let me not despise the smallest of Thy benefits, for but one of Thy blessings brings more than all the world could give.

For the lovely things this day, the good things, the true things,

I thank Thee, Lord.

For deeds of mercy, words of kindness, for every sign of sympathy and affection,

I thank Thee, Lord.

For the multitudes of men whose labours have brought me sustenance and comfort,

I thank Thee, Lord.

For renewal of my body, and new strength in mind and soul,
                              I thank Thee, Lord.

For forgiveness of my sins, and power to start afresh,
                              I thank Thee, Lord.

For Thy nearness to me now, and Thy Love still working for me,
                              I thank Thee, Lord.

For peace in heart and home,
                              I thank Thee, Lord.

Have pity on me, Lord God, for my strayings from Thy will. Give me a new heart, a changed mind. Change my way of thinking, until I have the Mind of Christ. Transform my way of living by the renewing of my mind. Give me the repentance which turns from darkness to light, the conversion which turns from serving self to serving Thee.

Make me a clean heart, O God, and renew in me a right spirit, Thy Spirit of Holiness. Though I seek, Good Lord, to be ever strong in body, heal first my soul. Thou requirest truth in the inward parts also, and wilt make me to be wise in the secret places of my soul. Purge me within. Then shall my soul rejoice, and my body know joy and gladness. I thank Thee, Father. Amen.

✠

Silent Meditation

Spirit of Love that dwells within, Spirit of Love that heals, I would trust myself to Thee.

THIRTY-FIRST DAY   *MORNING*

TEACH ME, Good Father, to lay all my troubles on Thee, to find them gone:

When my spirit is in heaviness, Thou knowest my path wherein I walk and lo! Thou liftest mine eyes to see that after all it ends in Thee;

When I have no place to flee unto, and no man cares for my soul, see! Thou art there, my sure abiding place;

When I look on my right hand and on my left, and my troubles compass me about, behold I am present with Thee, and am free;

When I am alone and in soreness of spirit, lo! Thou art my hope and my castle, my defender and deliverer, the lifter up of my head. Amen.

☧

Lord Jesus, Thou hast taught me that whatsoever I ask in Thy Name, the Heavenly father will grant it. Help me, then, to seek only that which can fitly bear Thy Name. I pray that what I say and do and think today may truly be called Christian. I pray that my desires and hopes and ambitions may not shame Thy purpose.

Make me to desire only what Thy Love can require, and as I seek Thy Presence now, help me to be a bearer of it throughout the day, that men may take knowledge of me that I have been with Thee, Jesus. Amen.

☧

Thou didst take flesh, Lord, to live for me;
Lord, I believe.

Thou didst do a craftsman's work, to sanctify my own;
                                        Lord, I believe.

Thou didst fashion a Cross, to carry it in triumph for my salvation;
                                        Lord, I believe.

Thou didst overflow with love for men with none;
                                        Lord, I believe.

Thou didst destroy death, to be with me for ever in life;
                                        Lord, I believe.

And, in this faith, I face the day. Amen.

☩

Silent Meditation

*I will be still, and know that in Thy
Presence is the fulness of Joy.*

☩

EVENING

LORD, Thou hast given me many hours of life and health and strength. Forgive me if I have used them ill. I confess that I am not worthy of the least of Thy mercies. But let not my sense of unworthiness draw a veil between me and Thee. Though Thou art hidden from my eyes, yet let my spirit discern Thee stirring within, ever renewing my life, ever at work to heal the wounds of sin and sickness. Before Time was, and beyond the end of it, Thy hand doth never cease its work of love.

At the close of day I give again the honour due unto Thy Name. Great Thou art, O Mighty Love; Thou canst not worthily be praised. Thanks be to Thee for Thy goodness. Amen.

O Great Father of Love, help me to deal with all the circumstances of this life with the hand of faith, and make my faith sure. Give me the faith that believes where I cannot understand, the faith that sees what these eyes see not, the faith that knows what the mind is ignorant of. Make me more and more aware that evil comes not from Thee, but from the absence of Thee.

And so I pray for a greater faith in Thee, a faith that goes on where there is no going, a faith which sees accomplished that which is not possible, a faith that gives wings to leaden feet, a faith that knows that Thou Art, and that there is none beside Thee. Dear Lord, Thou hast brought this faith to the very doors of my soul by the Power of the Risen Christ.

Give me grace now to open those doors on which He knocks, that He may come in and abide there. Thy Kingdom, O God, is at hand. Here I am, Lord, for Thy pleasure. Let Thy Kingdom come in me with great power. Do Thy will in me. Work Thy great work in me now. Behold, Thy Endless Life is given unto me. For ever and ever wilt Thou keep me. What should I fear in these short hours of Time? My faith is in Thee, Lord. At one with Thee I rest in peace, for Thy purpose for me shall surely be performed. Glory be to Thee, O Lord Most High. Amen.

✠

Silent Meditation

Be still, and know that I am Wisdom within thee;
sweetly and mightily I order all things in thee
to thy perfection.